The Kimchi Cookbook

THE Kimchi COOKBOOK

60 Traditional and Modern Ways to Make and Eat Kimchi

LAURYN CHUN

with Olga Massov

Photography by Sara Remington

TEN SPEED PRESS
Berkeley

Contents

FALL / WINTER KIMCHI 61

COOKING WITH KIMCHI 97

Acknowledgments

I would like to express my deepest gratitude to my *halmoni* (maternal grandmother), who instilled in me the foundations of cooking and my earliest memories of food; to my *umma* (mother), who taught me about the bounty of food and the importance of sourcing the highest-quality ingredients; to my *emo* (aunt) for always creating family celebrations around food; and to the *ajumas* (the ladies), and the entire staff at Jang Mo Jip restaurant in Garden Grove, California, who have been feeding everyone since 1989. I feel privileged to have had many enriching culinary and cultural experiences in my life, throughout my travels and among friends with whom I've shared meals, raised a glass of wine, cooked, and touched the dirt. Also, to the great chefs who've ignited my passion for food, from five-star dining experiences at Bouley, Gotham Bar and Grill, Le Bernardin, Daniel, Gramercy Tavern, the French Laundry, Jean Georges, and Arzak, to my introduction to the world of fine dining working at La Cachette in Los Angeles, to every countryside restaurant I dined at by happenstance in Europe and roadside food vendor I encountered throughout my travels in Southeast Asia. Their common language of food made an indelible impression on me. Each experience became a crucial building block and contributed to this book.

Thanks to my editor, Melissa Moore, for making this book possible with her courage and foresight, and for her patience in listening to my voice and vision even when I couldn't hear myself. Thanks also to Olga

Massov, my cowriter, for her enthusiasm for fish sauce, diligence, and teamwork, for keeping me on track in and out of the kitchen, and for letting the words take shape. To Jessica Boucher, Kristina Ratliff, Ryan Urcia, Tattfoo Tan, Bernard Sun, and countless others who, from the very beginning, helped ignite my desire to share kimchi with the world; and to my cousin Cathy Muma for sharing her new kitchen and testing the recipes, Hakyung Choi for all of her insights. Thanks to Betsy Stromberg, art director extraordinaire, and to Sara Remington for her beautiful photographs and enthusiasm, and for assembling a dream team with Katie Christ and Jaimi Holker. I won't forget Sara's dedication to our photoshoot, limping with an ice pack wrapped around her knee, yet a smile on her face showing love of all things kimchi. Thanks to Renato D'Agostin for my first official portrait and to Adam Field for providing *onggi* photographs; to Alan Tardi and Steven Hall for their timely feedback. To Norman Roberts for his unyielding patience and encouragement that allowed me to go after my dreams, a heartfelt thank you.

Thanks to Robert LaValva and the entire team and fellow vendors at New Amsterdam Market for providing the stage to be part of the regional, seasonal market community that served as catalyst to share the full story of kimchi. A special thanks to Fany Gerson, Justin V. Barocas, and Tara Q. Thomas for their faith in my story. And to every person and patron who showered me with their curiosity, interest, and excitement about Mother-in-Law's Kimchi and shared their personal stories about how they found their way to kimchi. Thank you for making possible my small dream of changing the world with one jar of kimchi at a time and for helping me to find my voice.

Introduction

I have been eating kimchi all my life. But I only truly smelled it about three years ago, when I was making kimchi alone for the first time. The vivid aromas suddenly brought me back to my childhood in Seoul, to my maternal grandmother and my earliest memories of food. I must have been about five years old, walking through the woods with my grandmother foraging for wild plants that would turn up at the dinner table; smelling the enticingly intense aroma of freshly roasted soybeans, used for making a fermented soybean paste called *doenjang*; tasting the warmth of a freshly laid egg; and watching a chicken from our backyard being butchered. Although we had moderate means, the act of preparing food formed a large part of my childhood, and especially of what gave me comfort. There was a sense of excitement watching my grandmother or mother in the kitchen preparing the food that would play a central role in bringing together the entire family at mealtime.

I also remember watching my grandmother make kimchi with the neighborhood *ajumas* (a respectful term for maternal figures, like madam or ma'am) during *kimjang*, the annual fall cabbage harvest, when I was six years old. From time to time, I'd run up to my grandmother, and she'd give me small pieces of the inner cabbage leaf with the rolled-up stuffing in them. It was always so special to me—a bond of love between us and a preview of the kimchi we would be eating all winter.

> The photo opposite shows our signature kimchi at various stages of fermentation. the bottom left bowl shows it fresh; the bottom right has been fermented 2 to 3 days; the top left has been fermented 1 week; and the top right has been fermented 1 month.

Suddenly it all made sense—why I was so curiously drawn to food and wine, my secret fascination when the deep smell of an aged red wine elicited a faint memory of roasted soybeans, the familiar intense meaty aroma of a properly made veal stock, the musky smell of wine cellars or

ripe cheese that made me recall the comforting memories of my childhood in Seoul, Korea. I had come full circle from my Korean roots, through Western traditions, culminating in rediscovering kimchi.

In Korea, kimchi is eaten with every meal. I was about eight years old when my family came to the United States, and, like many immigrant families, we spent a lot of time shopping for food and preparing what was going to be served on the table. There were always two shopping trips: I recall spending entire weekends shopping for Korean ingredients at specialty shops and then visiting typical American grocery stores. Our family dinners showcased my mother's innate ability to create endless delicious meals out of what we bought. While I was adapting to American culture, I was often embarrassed about how pungent Korean food is compared to American food, and I found myself ashamed and reluctant to share Korean traditions. Food was very important to us, and yet Korean food was so different, especially kimchi, so foreign, spicy, and stinky that it seemed as if it had no place in the American kitchen. I couldn't see a bridge between the two cultures.

My mother often cautioned me that kimchi was the one Korean tradition that would offend people because it is so pungent, and she warned me never to share kimchi with anyone who wasn't Korean. She told me kimchi was particularly not something I should eat in front of others, let alone take it for lunch to eat in public, and that I should always be mindful about kimchi's malodorous characteristics.

While growing up in Southern California, I often found myself straddling the two worlds—Korean and American—and trying to reconcile the food, culture, and language between the two seemingly contradictory cultures. The Korean world was a familiar one, while the American one seemed imposing and intimidating. In trying to understand where I fit between the two worlds, I struggled to find my voice.

My food journey was not a straight path. I attended college and, after graduation, chose not to pursue law school and instead dutifully found desk jobs. But I felt connected to my most authentic self when I was traveling abroad and discovering food. On a three-month backpacking trip through Europe, I was introduced to the food and wine cultures of Italy and France, which changed me forever. I was strangely comforted upon arriving at each new town, perusing the open-air food markets or grocery stores, discovering new cuisines, and tasting the local specialties. I realized that these seemingly foreign places were similarly deeply entrenched in culinary traditions similar to my Korean culture.

These pivotal experiences inspired me to launch a career in food and wine that included working as an assistant manager of an upscale French restaurant, organizing editorial tastings at a national wine magazine, managing a wine portfolio, and picking grapes for wine at a harvest in Italy. There were many times when I doubted my decision—I thought that kimchi and the pungent flavors of Korean food might have ruined my palate and spoiled my sense of smell, that it may have interfered with my ability to taste subtle flavors and appreciate the aroma of a fine vintage wine. I never imagined there could be common ground between kimchi and my love of the European food traditions that I held in such high regard, until that singular moment when I truly smelled kimchi for the first time. The bridge I had been looking for my entire life had been right under my nose all along.

My mother has operated Jang Mo Jip ("Mother-in-Law's House") restaurant in Garden Grove, California, since 1989. The restaurant business was not a planned career, but rather the result of dire necessity that grew out of a sad family event—the untimely passing of my father. My mother didn't have much time to grieve; she had a family to support. And thus the restaurant was born.

I've always been inspired by my mother's entrepreneurial success, but I didn't plan to follow in her footsteps by opening a Korean restaurant. And yet, at the restaurant, there was always a sense of comfort in a bowl of *seollungtang* soup—the house specialty beef brisket and bone mixture simmered in a cauldron overnight, a time-honored tradition of extracting the essence of the stock—and a side dish of kimchi. Traditionally this soup is particularly prized as a breakfast meal, although it is also eaten

> The term *Mother-in-law* has deep roots in Korean culinary culture. It refers to the tradition of a Mother-in-law spoiling a bridegroom with delicious food, as a sort of dowry, to convince him that his soon-to-be-wife's family cooking was top-notch. Also, in kimchi tradition, the bride would learn how to make kimchi, one of the most important culinary skills in Korea, from her new Mother-in-law as a gesture of devotion to her new family.

What do wine and kimchi have in common?
Those who taste kimchi for the first time often react to the level of spice, but its real defining characteristic is its tanginess. We often associate this sensation with sourness and acidity, but in kimchi, it's more than the flavor of vinegar— it's the taste of fermentation. It is a unique characteristic that all fermented foods, such as wine, beer, or cheese, share. The acidity produced by natural fermentation due to lactic acid is more natural for our own body's digestive pH and not as aggressive to our taste buds as the acidity in many commercially manufactured vinegars.

Texture and flavors. When the flavors of kimchi—chile pepper spice, garlic, and ginger— blend together in a perfect acidity (pH), the result is a delicate balancing act of flavors and sensations similar to what wine achieves. And in the same way, kimchi's vast array of differences in flavor and texture also depend on a balance of flavors and fermentation. The natural fermentation process helps flavors meld together with acidity and brightness that work to create the depth, roundness of texture, and complexity that develop with aging.

Balance. I often think of kimchi as the vegetable equivalent of German Riesling, because the variance of acidity, sugar, and texture in these wines exceeds any other. Contrary to many who think all Rieslings are sweet (or that all kimchi is too spicy), there is much more to the flavor than what we taste as sweet due to texture, acidity (pH), and the magic of fermentation.

Ageability. Like wine, which is always changing in the glass as well as in the bottle, kimchi is also always changing. And just like wine, there are some that taste better with age, like fall/winter root vegetable kimchi, and some that are meant to be eaten right away, like tender spring/summer vegetable kimchi. It's akin to the difference between a vintage red Bordeaux wine and a fresh white wine like Sauvignon Blanc.

The Champagne of pickles. Kimchi is a pickling tradition, and it tingles on the tongue like a sparkling wine with tiny pinpricks of carbonation. And just as each of France's famous Champagne houses has developed its own coveted blend of grapes and techniques to create its own unique style of sparkling wine, every Korean family has its own style of kimchi making, resulting in a finished kimchi all its own. No two families will agree that their kimchi is the same and they will remain loyal to their own family recipe.

Kimchi is perfectly captured in time—very much like wine. Kimchi and wine are living products, and therefore always changing. When you pour a glass of wine, the wine reacts to its exposure to oxygen and changes over time. In the same way, kimchi's colors, texture, flavors, and acidity are also affected by oxygen and aging. Its uniqueness is that it is a natural process, much like fermentation of wines and cheeses. It is not a stable, manufactured process, so each batch of kimchi will not taste exactly the same. Kimchi's individuality lies in the time, soil, climate, seasons, and even the location where the vegetables are grown. Each of these elements plays a role in fermentation and the final result.

throughout the day. The regulars, old neighborhood men, line up at 7 a.m. to be served the first bowl of piping hot, milky soup from the cauldron. I love seeing the many familiar faces of *ajumas,* who cook and operate the restaurant with the same care as if they were feeding their own families. The extended families with multiple generations that still visit our restaurant make an impression on me, especially when I see my mother greet each familiar face with a warm welcome. For 23 years, I had grown up eating kimchi from my mother's restaurant, and each time I went home to visit, she would send me back to New York with delicious kimchi carefully packed to take home in my luggage.

Then, in 2008, during the financial downturn, I suddenly lost one of my routine desk jobs and was facing unemployment. Instead of plunging headfirst into a job search, I felt as if I were at a crossroads—something had to change. During this time, I visited a dear friend in Barcelona. The trip rekindled my love for the flavors of traditional foods and the Spanish idea of tapas, or appetizers, and eating little bites of foods infused with a perfect assortment of flavor combinations and textures. The flavor combinations of briny seafood, rich meatiness, fresh vegetables—their tangy and savory mixture—made me recall the complexity of flavors in Korean cuisine. Suddenly a lightbulb turned on in my head. For the very first time, I started to really understand kimchi and see its similarities, rather than what had seemed like their stark differences, to the wine- and cheese-making traditions I was so passionate about. I wanted to share this newfound insight about the craft of kimchi and its connection to other Western food traditions with the world in a way that hadn't been done before. I wanted to help people understand the the labor, the time-honored methods, and the process of natural fermentation that make kimchi such a unique, healthful, compelling, and complex food. And with that, in the fall of 2009, I launched my small-batch kimchi business, Mother-in-Law's Kimchi (MILKimchi).

Named after my mother's restaurant and using the original kimchi recipe that was developed by the *ajumas,* Mother-in-Law's Kimchi is an homage both to my roots and to the authenticity that is found in every culinary tradition. There are, I realized, more similarities than differences among these traditions. They're embedded in the foods that nurture us.

When I began making kimchi, I didn't understand its complexities or the common thread between kimchi and other fermented foods such as wine, cheese, beer, and bread. But along the way, I was welcomed by many who understood fermentation's unique results and its health benefits. Selling kimchi at the New Amsterdam Market in New York City, a market that celebrates regional foods, gave me the opportunity and vision to create seasonal varieties of kimchi and introduce it in a truly authentic way. Having grown up in Southern California, it was easy to lose sight of the seasons as good produce was readily available year-round. But the northeastern climate reminded me of the seasonal history of kimchi. There were tender napa cabbage, green onions, young radishes, stuffed cucumbers, and water kimchi (similar to gazpacho) in the spring and summer, while whole pieces of vegetables such as stuffed napa cabbage and bachelor radish kimchi were available during the fall and winter. I didn't know how these flavors would be received, but I wanted to help people understand kimchi—that it is more than just napa cabbage and that there is a profound seasonal aspect to it. I wanted to help people who were not brought up on kimchi to develop a taste for its unique flavors and to appreciate its raw, probiotic benefits and the versatile ways that it could be used in cooking.

It's hard to imagine that I am writing a cookbook, hoping to bring the tradition of kimchi to a much wider audience. Now MILKimchi is a growing business, selling kimchi in specialty markets across the country. It's amazing to reflect on my journey as I think about my mother's admonition that kimchi was the one food that I should not share with anyone who wasn't Korean. Look, Mom, I am sharing kimchi with the world and now everyone is listening! I hope that this book will guide you with an overview of the versatility of kimchi and inspire you to create your own favorite recipe.

Kimchi 101

Kimchi is more than one type of recipe; it is one of the most versatile pickling techniques. There are more than 160 foundational recipes for kimchi, and every Korean family has its own version of the basic recipe based on their regional style, in which they take enormous pride. The word *kimchi* is derived from a combination of two Chinese characters meaning "salted vegetables." The first recorded mention of pickled radishes in Korea dates back to the twelfth century. It's no accident that the pickling technique for kimchi is similar to the pickling techniques of Eastern European and Russian sauerkraut-making and cabbage-fermenting traditions. All kimchi making involves four processes: brining, seasoning, fermenting, and storing.

The kimchi recipes in this book are organized by season, and are divided into two categories: spring/summer and fall/winter. The seasonality of kimchi is integral to its flavors and reflects the vegetables available—warm-weather kimchi is very delicate and light, while cold-weather kimchi's root vegetables are hearty with deep flavors. Since Korean winters are cold, the produce available and the types of kimchi prepared reflect the winter season, although refrigeration and industrialized farming now allow many vegetables to be available year-round. If you live in a warmer climate such as Florida or California where the growing season is much longer than that in colder areas, you can adjust your kimchi making accordingly.

Kimchi is regularly served as part of *banchan,* an array of dishes served alongside every Korean meal, from breakfast to dinner. A meal without kimchi is unthinkable; hence the Korean saying that "if you have kimchi and rice, you won't starve." But kimchi is more than just a side dish—its versatility also makes it an invaluable and flavorful ingredient in cooking. This book offers an entire chapter showcasing a variety of recipes you can transform by using kimchi as an ingredient. There are soups and salads, sandwiches and stews, and sauces and drinks. And that's just the tip of the iceberg. As you become more comfortable cooking with kimchi, you might create your own delicious recipes using your favorite ingredients—I certainly hope that you will.

Components of Kimchi Making

BRINING

> In Korea, using your hands to make kimchi is so prevalent that you can buy red-pink (to match red chili pepper flakes) "kimchi gloves" to use during kimjang (the November cabbage harvest and the kimchi making that follows). Also, in Korea we say you possess *sohn-mat*, when you mix with your hands so much that it's as if your hands, rather than your tongue, know how to taste.

A well-brined vegetable is critical to the flavor, texture, and balanced fermentation of kimchi. As a general rule, kimchi that requires long-term fermentation, such as those in the Fall/Winter chapter and others that are aged more than 3 months, use a liquid brine of salt and water, whereas kimchi that has a short-term fermentation, such as summer types and others intended to be consumed within 3 months or less, use a dry salt brine that is applied directly to the vegetables. Both methods break down the vegetables' cellulose walls and open their pores to allow the seasoning to better penetrate the vegetables.

Brining also acts as a catalyst for fermentation and it is believed that a gradual, slower process of salt absorption into vegetables, such as an overnight saltwater brine for a whole cabbage, ensures a deeper and more complex flavor and better texture. This is why the large cabbage halves used in Stuffed Cabbage Kimchi (page 93) and recipes for other kimchi stored for the winter call for an overnight (8- to 10-hour) brine. Look for a limp cabbage with bright yellow and green leaves as a sign of a well-brined cabbage. There is a saying in Korea that the cabbage should look like "its breath has been sucked out." This stands in stark contrast to a quick, dry salt brine, where the salt is sprinkled directly onto the vegetables and left to be absorbed for a shorter period of time, as in many of the spring/summer recipes. When using a dry salt method, you'll know the cabbage is ready when you see that it's sweating its liquid out, leaving its leaves glistening with tiny beads of moisture as the cure penetrates the cabbage walls.

Don't be concerned about the amount of salt used in the initial brine, because rinsing the brined vegetables with water is part of a critical process to stop the curing process. The result brings out a slightly sweet, saline quality of the vegetable, highlighting the true flavor of food that can be achieved when cooking with salt to taste.

SEASONING

The most important component of kimchi seasoning is chile pepper flakes, aka *gochugaru*. The fruitiness, earthiness, and spiciness of *gochugaru* is highly prized, so choose the very best quality you can find. The addition of fresh garlic and ginger amplifies the spice notes, while using seafood ingredients such as fermented anchovy sauce and salted shrimp builds layered, complex flavors. These ingredients are particularly important as foundations of building flavors, as kimchi was made without chile peppers up until the seventeenth century (see page 17). The absence of chile peppers doesn't necessarily make for dull kimchi flavors, as using a variety of seasonings made with seafood or other proteins and fresh ingredients creates piquant, clean flavors that showcase the natural fermented vegetables.

Once the ingredients are blended, the seasoning paste becomes a sauce, and the natural flavors of the vegetables will meld together with the seasoning paste to create an ongoing state of fermentation. Climate, regional variations, and accessibility to certain ingredients dictate many of the recipes for the seasonings in kimchi, and there is a great deal of variance among them. In southern Korea, where the climate is warmer, recipes call for more seafood and a more pungent style of seasoning overall to help preserve the kimchi, whereas in the north, where the climate is cooler and seafood isn't as readily available, beef broth and a less pungent style of seasoning are used.

> If you like your kimchi spicier, use a two-step process to help bind the dry ingredients: first, toss the brined cabbage with additional chili pepper flakes until well coated, then mix the vegetables with the seasoning paste until well combined. This helps layer the color and spiciness.

> In the absence of chili pepper flakes, you can add 1/2 pureed red bell pepper to make a mild, sweet version of kimchi.

Mixing the Ingredients

Stuffing vegetables, mixing seasonings, layering, and packing vegetables into containers just cannot be done with a kitchen tool. Use your hands to apply the seasoning and keep disposable or dedicated kimchi gloves for this purpose, as the chile peppers and salt might irritate your skin after prolonged contact.

For mixing, use bowls made of nonreactive materials, such as glass, stainless steel, and ceramic, as plastic bowls may pick up color and flavor from the chile pepper seasoning.

Throughout this book, I recommend using a mini food processor to mince and combine garlic, ginger, and chile pepper flakes, and to puree salted shrimp. If you do not have one handy, feel free to finely chop and mince the seasoning paste ingredients and combine them manually.

FERMENTING

Kimchi is alive and always changing. When preparing kimchi, keep in mind that this isn't "pickling" or "canning" per se. What you're creating isn't a static product; it is, in fact, alive and will continue to change over time—the natural process of fermentation. The term *ferment* is derived from the Latin word *fermentare*, which means to leaven, or *fervere*, to seethe, which refers to the conversion of carbohydrates, bacteria, and yeast, under anaerobic conditions (without oxygen), into organic acids that preserve food. The kimchi may, at first, if underfermented, taste bitter or sour, or give off an odor before becoming a tangy, delicious pickled vegetable. Kimchi can be appreciated during many different stages of fermentation, and the tastiest kimchi can range from a fresh, instant batch to a carefully aged stash. Let your taste buds be your guide. You might want to eat kimchi that's meant to be aged over time fresh instead. Or you might discover that something like Mother-in-Law's Signature Kimchi (page 82), which was traditionally eaten almost immediately, tastes better after it sits and ferments for a while.

Kimchi fermentation doesn't require the addition of a bacterial culture, as naturally occurring yeast in the vegetables are activated by lactobacillus (lactic acid), a beneficial bacteria for digestion that is produced during the initial fermentation phase. An ambient temperature of 65°F to 70°F helps accelerate fermentation during the initial phase, while a cooler temperature of 40°F to 55°F results in a slower fermentation period. I advocate an initial fermentation period of one to three days at room temperature before moving your kimchi into a cool refrigerator (38°F to 40°F) for long-term storage and fermentation. When you see tiny bubbles forming in the container, you'll know that the kimchi is on its way to proper fermentation. Alternatively, you may immediately place the kimchi in your refrigerator for the entire fermentation period, which can take from one to two weeks at a minimum, but it may take at least three times as long to achieve the same stages of fermentation. Cool, steady temperature is key to longevity in fermentation. Be mindful that if you underferment your kimchi or open the jar too soon and expose it to oxygen, it will taste bitter or "off" or have a slight chemical smell, but this is quite natural. If you wait a few more days, the kimchi should ferment further and the taste will be more rounded.

Lactic acid is produced during the initial fermentation phase, killing off harmful bacteria that is otherwise eliminated by pasteurization. The initial fermentation usually occurs within two to four days, depending on the climate, temperature, and type of vegetables. This is also the

RULES FOR FERMENTATION

With well-fermented kimchi, you'll be rewarded with a fizzing sound as you open the lid on a jar, showing proper fermentation, and you'll enjoy the sensation of carbonation as you bite into a tangy piece of kimchi.

1. Keep contents tightly packed, covered and submerged (no exposure to air).

2. Store kimchi in a cool, shady place (away from sunlight).

3. Do not open the container repeatedly, which exposes kimchi to oxygen. Each change in environment (temperature,

contact with oxygen) changes the condition of kimchi.

4. Be mindful that kimchi fermentation is best when the vegetables are tightly packed (versus loosely packed) into a jar.

5. Always keep a plate under your kimchi container to catch overflow/expansion during the initial phase of fermentation.

6. For long-term storage, keep your kimchi in a place where it won't be disturbed, such as the back of the refrigerator.

stage when lactic acid is most active and when much of the vegetable liquid "juice" is released—and when malodor (carbon dioxide) and lactic acid are produced, and some bubbling occurs. Bear in mind that this initial stage is the most critical part of the fermentation process, but it is also very volatile as well. The vegetables produce excess liquid from the conversion of sugars and production of lactobacillus, and the jar lids swell from internal built-up pressure from gases. Opening the jar will cause the bubbles to rise up. Each stage of fermentation has its own visual cue, from bright colors to a more subdued orange hue as the kimchi ages and ferments (think about how the color of a young, bright ruby red wine changes into a dark, garnet red as the wine ages).

During the initial stage of fermentation (the first few days), it's best not to open the jar as the most important fermentation activity occurs when lactic acid is actively produced, thus lowering the kimchi's acidity. Although I recommend a room temperature of 65°F to 70°F for the initial fermentation stage, I am not accounting for altitude (which could extend the time needed for fermentation because of the atmospheric pressure difference), the temperature inside individual homes, or unforeseen climatic conditions, so be mindful about these conditions. If you want to work in a controlled refrigeration temperature (36°F to 40°F), you may do so, but take into consideration that the initial fermentation stage will be slower— seven to ten days versus two to three days at room temperature. Once the initial fermentation is complete, you can move the kimchi to a refrigerator, where it will continue to ferment slowly at a steady colder temperature. If, however, you have outdoor access and it's cold outside, you may keep your kimchi outside if you can protect it from freezing or high temperatures.

Techniques such as certain cuts for vegetables (ranging from small, bite-size pieces to larger chunks) or leaving vegetables whole can speed up or delay fermentation. Chopping cabbage into long strips, like we do in our signature kimchi (page 82), or into square shapes, as with Square-Cut Napa Cabbage Kimchi (page 78), accelerates fermentation, while keeping cabbages whole delays the speed of fermentation for months. Using salt, whether in a dry brine for short fermentation or in a wet brine for long-term fermentation, also plays a critical role in kimchi making. (See page 18 for more on salt's role.)

› You should see some bubbling in the juices without having to open the lid. Once properly fermented, open the jar and taste the kimchi; you will taste the tanginess of the freshly pickled cabbage. Try to remember the flavor and keep tasting your kimchi as it ages—the flavor will evolve and change with time. Make sure that your kimchi stays at a temperature between 36°F and 40°F to ensure an even, slow fermentation. That way, your kimchi should last up to a year.

Bear in mind that when working in batches and jarring your kimchi, fermentation will be better when the vegetables are packed tightly. This helps to achieve a more consistent fermentation, especially when working with large stuffed cabbage halves—the less oxygen there is in the jar and the tighter it's packed, the better the overall flavors that will develop.

A container with a tight-fitting lid works best for storing kimchi. When opening a lid, be mindful of the pressure that has built up inside the jar during the first fermentation. A layer of vegetable juice is often produced, which may overflow as the contents of the jar settle. It's best to keep gaps of air inside jars to a minimum, so pack your kimchi tightly. If you have premature fermentation, caused by excess air, you will note the off-putting odor and the vegetable will taste bitter. Although fermented foods have a certain briny smell to them, rotting foods are an altogether different matter. Perfectly brined food will yield a bright acidic note on your nose, whereas a brining batch gone awry will smell dull. You will notice the difference with your nose.

Resist the urge to open your containers of kimchi to check on them during fermentation, as contact with oxygen changes the state of fermentation. For example, with kimchi composed of large pieces of cabbage, the top layer might darken to a brownish hue. The discoloration is a result of oxidation—a natural chemical reaction—and not an indication of spoilage. Once it comes into contact with oxygen, kimchi's fermentation environment changes. This is something you want to avoid (traditionally one used a top layer of cabbage leaves to serve as a barrier).

Because fall/winter kimchi requires a longer fermentation period and more patience as you wait for it to age and develop layers of flavors, it can seem a bit intimidating at first. After all, how do you know when something is really fermented? What does it mean to have kimchi that is *truly* balanced in taste? As you taste more kimchi and begin to get a feel for how kimchi is *supposed* to taste, you will also become familiar with how kimchi changes with time. It may make sense for you to start with a few easy summer kimchi recipes: the spinach and mushroom salad (page 34), or the Quick Cucumber and Chive Kimchi (page 41), or perhaps deconstructed eggplant (page 57). You should try the various recipes in the seasonal chapters and get a feel for the type of kimchi

> A note about fermentation gone awry: Oxidation can wreak havoc on your fermentation, which is why it's important to keep the kimchi submerged in its briny seasoning. If you see even the slightest appearance of mold, remove the top layer and ensure that the remaining kimchi is totally covered.

flavors you like—milder or more pungent; liquid types; or crunchy or aged. You will find the right balance of flavors for you and will be well on your way to discovering your favorite types. In the Fall/Winter chapter, start with Square-Cut Napa Cabbage Kimchi (page 78) and build your way up to the Stuffed Cabbage Kimchi (page 93). As you move into longer fermented kimchi, you will gain confidence in your skills and have guaranteed success on your hands.

STORING

The most famous kimchi containers are the traditional earthenware pots called *onggi*, which were filled with kimchi and buried in the ground for the duration of winter. During the summer, they were placed under straw

> A typical kimchi *onggi*, which holds 33 gallons.

hut shelters for shade or in wells to protect them from the heat. *Onggi* were sculpted out of dark clay (or wood in mountanous areas) and prized for their microporous properties, which aid in the fermentation of food. Prior to refrigeration, most Korean families had backyards or designated areas where the *onggi* were placed, as they were considered an essential part of the home. These indispensable containers were used for a variety of fermented foods, from soybeans to chile paste to soy sauce, but only kimchi *onggi* are buried. Their sizes and shapes varied greatly, ranging from short to tall and from round to oblong, and the largest could hold up to 65 gallons.

Today, with refrigeration and urban living, most Korean city dwellers don't have enough room for one *onggi*, never mind several. The best substitutes are all-purpose glass jars or flat rectangular plastic containers with a tight seal that allows the contents to be tightly packed with kimchi. There are also special "kimchi refrigerators" for storing kimchi long-term, acting as modern day *onggi*. These refrigerators have a tight seal and are compartmentalized to control temperature. My mother tells me, however, that *onggi*-fermented kimchi has much deeper flavors, due to its interaction with the soil and outside climate through the porous clay material of the *onggi*.

I find that a glass container with a tight-fitting lid works well, as do plastic containers; cylindrical plastic containers with tight lids and especially rectangular varieties both work well as they are ideally suited for napa cabbage halves, which require a wide-mouthed opening. For kimchi cut into smaller pieces, pint- and quart-size glass jars (such as Ball or mason jars) are perfectly suitable. Remember to leave about one inch of space on top for the fermentation liquid to rise.

You may also want to consider using resealable bags or plastic bags that can be tied tightly, as long as you remove as much air as possible from them before sealing and keep them tightly sealed. (The safest bet is to double-wrap them in plastic.) The bags will bloat from the gas buildup, which is an indication of proper fermentation, and you want to be sure that they will hold up to the gas pressure. Just be sure to not let the contents have contact with air until the initial fermentation stage has occurred. You may then transfer the contents to a jar and refrigerate. Keep your kimchi stored at a consistant, cool temperature, and avoid contact with direct sunlight.

Whatever storage method you use, preventing the contents of the container from having contact with oxygen is of utmost importance.

The Kimchi Pantry

The basic components of a kimchi pantry are critical ingredients that, together, make the seasoning and fermentation foundation for kimchi. While chile peppers are the predominant spice and often the most visible ingredient, other items, such as anchovy sauce and salted shrimp, play an important role not only for flavor but also in the fermentation process. Sweet Rice-Flour Porridge (page 24) is added to some kimchi to increase viscosity and act as a binding agent in water kimchi, but is typically used for long-term kimchi fermentation. A well-balanced kimchi should taste unique when correctly balanced, with a layered, nuanced combination of spiciness, acidity, and texture. It will continue to improve its flavors as it ages—not like a vegetable that's been masked in seasonings with spicy heat, salt, or one dominant flavor.

Seasoning

When preparing the seasoning paste for your kimchi, it's helpful to think of the paste as a roux that is mixed with the brined vegetables, binding the vegetables and the seasonings together, transforming their flavors. Much like pasta sauce clings to starchy pasta to create one single unified dish, so do the brined vegetables and seasoning become kimchi.

DRIED KOREAN CHILE PEPPER FLAKES (*GOCHUGARU*)

Contrary to popular belief, Korean chili peppers are less spicy (about one-third less) than the tropical variety used in Southeast-Asian cooking (Thailand, Vietnam, and India) or the Mexican varieties. They are in the medium heat index and their earthy, fruity undertones make up an important flavor profile for kimchi that cannot be replicated by any other type of chile pepper. The common name for these peppers is Holland Reds, and these vibrant red peppers are between four and six inches in length and most commonly used as dried flakes (*gochugaru*). Used in many Korean dishes, they are the basis for much of kimchi seasoning and one of its most critical ingredients; try to find the highest quality available. Look for vibrant red coarse pepper flakes, as a brownish-red color is a sure sign of oxidation, which you want to avoid. You might see other grind sizes at specialty stores, but all of the recipes in this book use coarse grind red pepper flakes. Store *gochugaru* in an airtight container to avoid oxidation and keep it in the refrigerator or freezer to shield it from direct sunlight and retain its freshness.

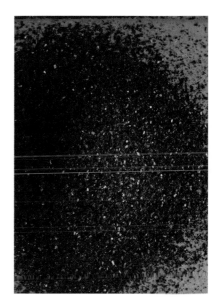

Before chile peppers were introduced to Korean cooking in the seventeenth century, kimchi was made with fermented salted seafood, proteins, or meat broths as seasoning. You will note that several of the recipes in this book, such as White Wrapped Kimchi with Persimons and Dates (page 73), are made without the use of the chile peppers. Those recipes are some of the oldest kimchi recipes to be found. However, the addition of peppers hasn't just enhanced kimchi's flavors. They also play a role in long-term fermentation as capsaicin, the chemical compound in chile that makes it spicy and also prevents white film bacteria growth and sustains acidity during long-term fermentation.

CHILE PEPPER THREADS (*SHIL GOCHU*)

Chile pepper threads are used throughout Korean cooking as a decorative element. They are reddish brown when dried, measure 2 to 3 inches long, and have a mildly spicy, smoky flavor.

SALTED SHRIMP (*SAEUJOT*)

Tiny salted and pickled shrimp called *saeujot* are a cornerstone of Korean cuisine. Pickling shrimp parallels the tradition of pickling herring or fish in Southeast Asia. Salted shrimp is used as a flavoring in many types of dishes as it is pungent but gives savory notes. When seeking out good-quality salted shrimp, look for clear, translucent bodies suspended in a luminous liquid.

ANCHOVY SAUCE (*JEOTGAL*)

> › Did you know that fish sauce has roots in ancient Western cultures? The Romans used a fermented fish sauce called *garum*. Fish sauce is a key ingredient across cultures because it has the same chemical component as *glutamate* in tomatoes and other umami-rich foods, such as shiitake mushrooms, seaweed, and even napa cabbage. Kimchi is an umami-rich food, as it combines the glutamate-enriched seasonings and vegetables with the process of fermentation that brings out their amino acids.

Although fish sauce is well represented throughout Southeast Asia, with the most popular being from Thailand and Vietnam, it varies greatly in flavor from region to region. Korean fermented anchovy sauce has softer undertones and is mellower than its Southeast Asian cousins. *Jeotgal* is responsible for much of the umami (a Japanese word that roughly translates as "delicious essence") notes in kimchi.

Salted shrimp and anchovy sauce are the most common seafood ingredients used for making kimchi, but regional styles use varieties of pickled corbina, oysters, sardines, or squid as seasonings. These fermented proteins add a roundness to offset what we taste as acidity and add complex savory notes. For an alternative to anchovy sauce, substitute a flavorful Mushroom Broth (page 26), which can also be used instead of salted shrimp. It's an earthy broth that is a great flavor enhancer. Also, consider using apple puree to give a sweet, crisp acidity to the flavor profile.

SALT (*SEOGUM*)

Salt—particularly coarse sea salt—is the foundation for preserving food in every culture, and it is a key component for making kimchi. Salt is deeply prized by Koreans for its ability to preserve foods. Proper salting is essential for the vegetables to absorb the seasonings, resulting in a delicious, balanced kimchi. Although an ample amount of salt is used for brining, most of the salt is rinsed off prior to incorporating the seasoning paste. It is commonly believed that a wet-brined cabbage, as opposed to dry-brined cabbage, will develop deeper flavors during fermentation.

The role of salt brining is to open the pores of the vegetables and to act as a catalyst for fermentation. By breaking down vegetables' walls with salt, the vegetables better absorb the seasonings and ferment more evenly.

Since salt granules vary in size from type to type and manufacturer to manufacturer, a teaspoon of salt from one maker will amount to a different weight/quantity than a teaspoon of salt in another maker—this can affect your results either by over- or underseasoning your kimchi. For consistency in this book, we used Diamond Crystal Kosher Salt exclusively, as it was more readily accessible than large quantities of coarse sea salt (which is what would traditionally be used for kimchi). If you do have access to large quantities of sea salt (available at Korean markets), please adjust salt amounts according to taste when following the recipes—coarse sea salt has larger crystals than kosher salt, and is less salty teaspoon for teaspoon, so you'll need additional amounts in order to create the proper salinity for fermentation. As a guideline, keep in mind that a proper wet brine should have a salinity similar to ocean water.

GARLIC (MANUL)

Use fresh garlic, minced or pureed using a mini food processor, to form a paste-like consistency. Don't be heavy-handed with garlic, as too much garlic in kimchi can make the overall flavor too bitter.

GINGER (SAENGGANG)

Use fresh ginger, using a teaspoon to scrape away the skin (it works better than a vegetable peeler), and either chop it finely or puree it using a mini food processor. As a general guideline, the ratio of ginger to garlic should be 1:2 in kimchi recipes.

SUGAR (SULTANG)

Although sugar is not the most likely ingredient one would imagine using when fermenting vegetables, it is necessary in order to balance the flavors of different vegetables, particularly during fermentation. Dense vegetables

› The ingredients in kimchi reflect the five-color principle found in Korean culinary culture. The five colors—white, red, green, brown, and yellow—represent the sky, earth, fire, wind, and rain and are often found in Korean dishes.

like daikon radishes require a bit more sugar than others, and overall I find that not using enough sugar leads to kimchi with bitter, sour notes. Use your own judgment as to how much sugar to use—add an extra teaspoon or use a teaspoon less, depending on your taste. If you want to avoid using sugar altogether, substitute pureed apple, pear, or sweet onion to taste.

Vegetables

As a traditionally agrarian society, Koreans take great pride in and care of their vegetables and the land on which they're grown. They have a reverence for vegetables and source the best ingredients at their seasonal peak to prepare kimchi.

NAPA CABBAGE (*BAECHU*)

From the Japanese word *nappa,* which refers to the leaves of a vegetable, napa cabbage is traditionally grown all over Asia and is the anchor of kimchi ingredients. It is prized for its soft, fleshy, juicy leaves, which retain water well. It is vastly different from the round western cabbage, which tends to have a lower water content and more fibrous texture. Napa cabbage's delicate texture marries well with fermentation, resulting in a tangy, carbonated sensation. Look for a cabbage ranging between 2 and 3 pounds with bright light green, sturdy leaves, a tight core, and creamy flesh. Napa cabbage is such a tender, soft cabbage that it loses about 25 percent of its volume during the kimchi process. Unlike the more durable round western cabbages that can endure colder temperatures, napa cabbage has a shorter growing season. From White Stuffed Cabbage Kimchi (page 89), to Square-Cut Napa Cabbage Kimchi (page 78), to Mother-in-Law's Signature Kimchi (page 82), napa cabbage is used widely in kimchi making. It's no wonder when people think of kimchi, they think of napa cabbage. In general, it isn't necessary to thoroughly wash napa cabbage before making kimchi, since the brining process involves a lot of rinsing.

KOREAN CHIVES (*BUCHU*)

With their flat ramp-like leaves and mild garlicky scent, Korean chives (also called Korean leeks) are somewhat different than European chives and look more like long, flat blades of grass. Commonly called *buchu*, Korean chives can be used on their own as in Chive Kimchi (page 54), or as a stuffing ingredient in something like Stuffed Cucumber Kimchi (page 37). Green onions or European chives work well as a substitute, if you're not able to find Korean chives.

DAIKON RADISH (*MUU*)

Daikon radish is the most popular vegetable for kimchi after napa cabbage, and it is as common in Korean cooking as a carrot is in the West. Daikon radish is a general term for the vast array of radishes grown all over Asia; they can range from 6 to 18 inches in length and can weigh from 1 to 4 pounds. They are eaten throughout Asia and are enjoyed cooked, pickled, or raw. The root is white, dense, and juicy, and the greens are a vibrant green. Their flavors vary greatly. The most notable characteristic of daikon radish is its refreshing texture, much like a jicama, with mildly spicy finishing notes that vary depending on the size and type. From the young radishes used in Bachelor Radish Kimchi (page 87) to the mature daikon radish used in Daikon Radish Cube Kimchi (page 85) to tender, small daikon radishes pickled in clear broth (page 95) to the tiny root-like daikon radishes in Korean Radish Top Kimchi (page 48), the variety of daikon radishes is stunning, and it is as prized for its greens as it is for its root. Different radish kimchi recipes require different types of daikon, and you can find a wide variety at a Korean market. Farmers' markets may also offer more varieties of radishes than a supermarket. When shopping, look for shorter, stout radishes (which tend to be crunchier) rather than longer ones.

It's important to rinse radishes. Using a vegetable brush, clean the dirt off the radish skins, but do not peel the outer layer. The skins provide an important layer of protection, preventing the radishes from getting soft during the long fermentation period.

Cutting Shapes

Beyond sourcing the proper vegetables, cutting and shaping them correctly plays an important role in kimchi recipes (Refer to the photo, at right).

Nabak (lower left and center)—A thin, flat, square shape that is bite-size at 1¹/₂ to 2 inches, nabak is used for both napa cabbage and daikon radishes in many kimchi, from ready-to-eat water kimchi (pages 43 and 67) to Wrapped Seafood Kimchi (page 76) and Square-Cut Napa Cabbage Kimchi (page 78). To cut napa cabbage into the nabak shape, halve the cabbage vertically, then cut each piece in half to make quarters. Cut out the core from each piece, then cut each into 2-inch squares that are as uniform as possible.

Gutjori (see photo page 46)—These mostly long, strip cuts are made specifically for the fresh/instant kimchi style. I prefer this rough cut as it allows longer and more even fermentation. Keeping the length to 3 to 4 inches is a key for many kimchi recipes that feature young vegetables, such as Korean Radish Top Kimchi (page 48) and Tender Young Napa Cabbage Kimchi (page 47).

Stuffed/Whole/Halved (upper left)—The idea of making incisions and stuffing vegetables is central to many Korean kimchi recipes. Keeping vegetables whole or halved slows fermentation, and supports the traditional concept of tasting the vegetable intact, bringing the ideal balance of flavor.

Cubes (upper right)—These bite-size 1 to 1¹/₂ inch cubes are specific to Daikon Radish Cube Kimchi (page 85).

Matchsticks (far right)—Thin, delicate matchsticks are the most common cut used for daikon radish when it will be used as stuffing.

Foundational Recipes

The staples recipes included on the following pages are key ingredients to help bind the seasoning paste as well to add flavor and thicken the overall texture of kimchi. Adding the following recipes to your repertoire will take your kimchi to great heights.

Sweet Rice-Flour Porridge

A staple of kimchi paste ingredients, this porridge acts as a binding agent and makes the seasoning more viscous. The starchiness of this porridge helps offset the bitterness of certain vegetables used for kimchi. It takes only minutes to make, and will keep for a few days in the refrigerator—ready for spur-of-the-moment kimchi making. It's an easy recipe to double or triple, if you'd like to have a lot on hand.

› Cooking time: 20 minutes (includes ice-bath cooling time) › Makes about 1 cup

1 cup cold water
2 tablespoons sweet rice flour

Prepare an ice bath. In a small saucepan, bring $3/4$ cup of the water to a boil. Meanwhile, dissolve the flour in the remaining $1/4$ cup of cold water. Whisk the flour mixture into the boiling water and stir for 15 to 30 seconds, until the mixture thickens and resembles white glue. Remove from the heat and set in the ice bath to cool. When cool, remove from the ice bath. Allow to come to room temperature, stirring, 5 to 10 minutes. If making ahead, transfer the mixture to a container and refrigerate until needed. The porridge will keep for up to 3 days, refrigerated.

Beef Stock

This basic beef stock is made using beef brisket, though stew meat such as chuck or skirt steak will also work. It's simmered for 2 hours and can be used throughout cooking in many Korean dishes as a soup stock and also as a seasoning base. The brisket is often cooked with a seasoning sauce then used as topping for soups. If you have plenty of stock left over, you can use it as a base for kimchi soup or serve it with the kimchi dumplings (page 109).

> Cooking time: **about 2 hours** > Makes 4 quarts

1¹/₂ pounds beef brisket
6 quarts cold water

Rinse the beef brisket, place it in a large stockpot, and cover with cold water. Cook uncovered over medium-high heat, until the water comes to a boil. Reduce the heat to low and simmer for about 2 hours, skimming off the fat regularly, until reduced by a third and a light stock forms. Remove the brisket and reserve for another use. Let the stock cool, then refrigerate and use within 2 days or freeze for up to 6 months.

Shredded Beef in Seasoning Sauce

Use this seasoning sauce on the beef brisket that's left after making the beef stock. You can then use the shredded beef to make soft tacos or add it to quesadillas and salads.

Makes 10 cups

- ¹/₄ cup soy sauce
- 3 tablespoons toasted sesame oil
- 3 green onions, white and green parts, chopped (about ¹/₃ cup)
- 2 tablespoons finely chopped garlic
- ¹/₂ teaspoon freshly ground black pepper
- 3 teaspoons toasted sesame seeds (optional)

Follow the recipe above for making beef stock. Remove the cooked beef brisket from the stock and lay it on cutting board to cool for 15 to 20 minutes.

Meanwhile, in a large bowl, combine the soy sauce, sesame oil, green onions, garlic, black pepper, and toasted sesame seeds and set aside. Cut any remaining fat from the beef and, while it's still warm to the touch, shred the beef into matchstick-size pieces using your hands. In a bowl, mix the sauce and shredded beef until well combined. Serve at room temperature or refrigerate, covered, for up to 4 days.

Mushroom Broth

For vegetarians or vegans, here is a flavorful mushroom broth to use as an alternative to anchovy sauce and salted shrimp. While the flavor won't be an exact match, the earthiness and round undertones of mushrooms will help the kimchi achieve those subtle complex notes. Bear in mind that the broth is highly salted to bring out the mushroom essence and to replace the salt found in the anchovy sauce and salted shrimp. So when making your kimchi, taste and adjust the seasonings as you like.

This recipe can be easily doubled or tripled or increased to make any amount you need.

› Cooking time: 20 minutes   › Makes about 1 cup

$^1/_4$ cup dried shiitake or porcini mushrooms
1 cup boiling water
1 tablespoon kosher salt

Place the mushrooms in a medium bowl. Pour the boiling water over the mushrooms. Stir in the salt. Cover and let sit for 20 minutes. Squeeze the water out of the mushrooms and allow the broth to cool to room temperature or refrigerate before using. Discard the mushrooms or store them in the broth to further infuse their flavor. Refrigerate, covered, for up to 2 weeks.

TIP

You can use a combination of pureed apples, pears, or onions and sea salt to achieve similar salty notes and make a vegan version of any kimchi. I recommend a ratio of 1 teaspoon salt per $^1/_2$ cup of puree. You may also use dried seaweed in place of the mushrooms to achieve a similar broth.

Naturally Vegan Kimchi

You can adjust nearly all of the kimchi recipes in this book to be vegan. If you don't want to substitute ingredients, go straight to these recipes that are fully vegan:

- Tri-Colored Bell Pepper and Cabbage Water Kimchi in Clear Broth (page 42)

- Korean "Gazpacho" Water Kimchi in Red Pepper Broth (page 43)

- French Breakfast Radish Kimchi (page 51)

- Cipollini Onion Kimchi (page 56)

- Cauliflower Water Kimchi with Turnip, Lime Zest, and Pomegranate in Clear Broth (page 67)

- Butternut Squash Kimchi with Lacinato Kale and Pine Nuts (page 69)

- Savoy Cabbage Kimchi with Turnip (page 80)

SPRING / SUMMER KIMCHI

After a long winter, early signs of spring bring excitement, especially when the first of the season's green vegetables appear—green onions, radishes, lettuce, and tender napa cabbage. They reflect the bounty of spring vegetables at their best and are often consumed quickly. Spring and summer kimchi celebrates fresh produce at its peak; it's not preserved for long. Unlike the winter kimchi, which takes time to ferment, the seasonings in spring and summer kimchi are applied with a much lighter touch in order to enhance the flavor of the tender vegetables. These warm-weather kimchi are often eaten immediately or within a few days. The brining methods are quick, dry-salt methods in which the salt is sprinkled directly on the vegetables, opening the pores of the vegetables and preparing them for the seasoning intake. Most of these kimchi recipes are quick and simple, and the fermentation process only lasts anywhere from a few minutes—essentially a dressed salad—to a few days. Their common traits are quick fermentation, lightness, and juiciness—the liquid is a broth that complements the seasoning nicely.

Much as watermelon signals the arrival of summer to some people, these four types of kimchi say "summer" to me: tender napa cabbage, or *putbaechu* (page 47); tender daikon radish roots, or *yeolmu* (page 48); stuffed cucumbers, or *oi sobagi* (page 37); and gazpacho kimchi, or *nabak baechu mulkimchi* (page 43). These seasonal treats typically appear at every mealtime, a sign that summer has finally arrived. These kimchi are very refreshing, perfect for the humid, hot summers of Korea, where a bowl of rice or cold noodles and *banchan*—an assortment of flavorful side dishes with spicy, savory pickled vegetables and kimchi—can make up an entire meal.

Putbaechu is a tender, young cabbage that is delicate and subtle, more like a lettuce than a cabbage, with light flavors and juice that make it wholly refreshing. *Yeolmu* is a tiny, tender white daikon radish with long stems that is prized for its celery-like crispness. *Mulkimchi*, which means "water kimchi," has a flavor like gazpacho—the ultimate refreshment in the summer. A chilled water soup, mulkimchi offers bite-size square-cut (*nabak*) shapes of radishes and vegetables in an invigorating broth. You may want to drink this cold soup with every meal, or use it as a base for a savory cocktail—think pickle brine in picklebacks. Its flavors are a stark contrast to the heavy fermented flavors of winter kimchi, as they capture the lightness of sunny days. They are a celebration of the season with flavors that complement the warm weather.

An all-time summer favorite is the Stuffed Cucumber Kimchi (page 37), which is a melding of chile peppers and chives that marries nicely with refreshing juicy cucumbers. Kids love them and it's a fun and easy recipe to make. I recall making this cucumber kimchi with my mother every summer. The kimchi juice from the stuffed cucumbers is especially good for a summer cocktail or quick snack of rice noodles in cold kimchi soup. For an even easier kimchi recipe, try the Quick Cucumber and Chive Kimchi (page 41) as a fast side dish with instant bright flavors to accompany any summer main dish.

The Deconstructed "Stuffed" Eggplant Kimchi (page 57) celebrates eggplant, another summer treat. Stuffing (called *sobagi*) is a technique that is used throughout kimchi making, especially for small vegetables, where you place stuffing into slits cut into the vegetable. I decided to take the dish apart, by tossing pieces of eggplant with a seasoning paste. By exposing more surface area of the eggplant to the seasoning paste, it cures more effectively. It turned out to be one of my favorite recipes in the book—the refreshing eggplant flavor paired with an unexpectedly spicy seasoning makes this an excellent accompaniment to grilled chicken, salads, or for a fresh mozzarella sandwich.

The key to summer kimchi is to make it often and enjoy it right away—there is no need to make a huge batch for season-long consumption. As you become more comfortable with quick summer pickles, try moving beyond the vegetables featured in this chapter and experiment with your own seasonal produce. The possibilities are endless, and since the fermentation time is so short, it's easy to experiment with different vegetables and create your own favorites.

Instant Red Leaf Lettuce Kimchi

Sang-Chu Gutjori (TRADITIONAL)

Find the most tender fresh lettuce at your local farmers' market, and make this tossed salad that's similar to a salsa and perfect for showcasing Kimchi seasoning. Serve it alongside grilled flank steak at your next barbecue or weekday dinner. Think of it as a shortcut to Korean barbecue, as the kimchi seasoning acts as a vinaigrette with unmistakeable Korean flavors.

› Prep: 20 minutes › Fermentation: Ready to eat › Makes 8 to 10 cups (serves 4 to 6)

1 head (about 8 ounces) red leaf lettuce

Seasoning Paste
2 tablespoons Korean chile pepper flakes
2 tablespoons anchovy sauce
1 teaspoon chopped garlic

1/2 red bell pepper, cut into 1-inch slivers
    (about 2/3 cup)
2 green onions, green parts only, sliced diagonally
    (about 2 tablespoons)
2 tablespoons thinly sliced red onion
1 teaspoon toasted sesame oil (optional)
1 teaspoon toasted white sesame seeds (optional)

Soak the lettuce in water to remove any dirt, then trim the leaves into 2-inch sections and discard the ends. Set the lettuce aside to air-dry, or use a salad spinner to spin-dry the leaves.

Meanwhile, to make the seasoning paste, mix together the chile pepper flakes, anchovy sauce, and garlic in a small bowl. Set aside for 10 minutes to let the flavors combine.

In a medium bowl, toss the lettuce with the bell pepper and the green and red onions. Dress the salad with the seasoning paste. Drizzle with the sesame oil and sprinkle with the sesame seeds. Serve immediately.

Instant Baby Spinach and Oyster Mushroom Kimchi

Shigumchi Bauesut Gutjori (CONTEMPORARY)

This is another example of instant kimchi—something you can make quickly and enjoy immediately. Baby spinach is lovely and delicate, and mushrooms readily absorb all the flavors of the dressing. Think of this salad as flavorful and satisfying with meaty, earthy mushroom notes. Once tossed, let the salad sit for ten minutes or so to allow the flavors to blend together. The spinach wilts slightly, yielding to the spicy kimchi paste. Serve this salad as an alternative to your typical spinach salad, alongside some pan-seared salmon or grilled fish.

› Prep: 20 minutes › Fermentation: Ready to eat › Makes 8 cups (4 to 6 servings)

8 cups (about 6 ounces) baby spinach
5 ounces oyster, enoki, or cremini mushrooms
1/3 cup thinly sliced red bell pepper
1/4 cup thinly sliced red onion

Dressing
1 tablespoon Korean chile pepper flakes
1 teaspoon anchovy sauce (optional)
1/2 teaspoon minced garlic
1/2 teaspoon peeled, finely grated fresh ginger
1 teaspoon sugar
1 tablespoon Sweet Rice-Flour Porridge (page 24)

Wash and thoroughly dry the spinach, and place in a large bowl. Using a damp towel or a vegetable brush, wipe the mushrooms clean. Thinly slice the mushrooms and transfer to the bowl with the spinach. Add the bell pepper and onion.

To make the dressing, in a small bowl, combine the chile pepper flakes, anchovy sauce, garlic, ginger, and sugar to make a paste. Stir in the porridge.

Toss the vegetables with the dressing. Set aside for at least 10 minutes to let the flavors combine. Refrigerate the leftovers and consume within 1 day.

Bok Choy Kimchi

Chung Kyong Chae (CONTEMPORARY)

Bok choy, the well-known Chinese cabbage, looks a lot like a mini napa cabbage. It is great for summertime kimchi, needing only a short fermentation period to highlight its crisp texture. In this recipe, we've halved the bok choy lengthwise, to preserve a traditional look. However, feel free to cut the ends and separate the leaves in order to toss them together.

› Prep: 1 hour › Brine: 45 minutes › Fermentation: Ready to eat, or 1 day, depending on your preference › Makes 4 cups (4 to 6 servings)

Brine
1 pound bok choy, halved lengthwise
4 cups water
2 tablespoons kosher salt

Seasoning Paste
1 1/2 tablespoons Korean chile pepper flakes
1 tablespoon anchovy sauce
1 teaspoon sugar
1 teaspoon minced garlic
1/2 teaspoon peeled, finely grated fresh ginger

10 sprigs European chives, or 2 green onions, green part only, cut into thin diagonal slivers (about 1/4 cup)
1/2 medium carrot, peeled and julienned into 3-inch strips (about 1/4 cup)
1/4 red bell pepper, julienned into 3-inch strips (about 3 tablespoons)

Trim the bok choy ends and discard any wilted or yellow leaves. Wash the bok choy by soaking it in several changes of water, being careful to remove any dirt that's trapped under the leaves. In a large bowl, combine the water with the salt. Soak the bok choy in the brine for 45 minutes. Rinse the bok choy with cold water to remove all traces of the salt, and let drain in a colander for 15 to 20 minutes.

Meanwhile, make the seasoning paste. In a small bowl, stir together the ingredients. Set aside for 15 minutes to let the flavors combine.

In a large bowl, combine the seasoning paste with the chives. Add the bok choy, carrot, and bell pepper, and thoroughly mix, making sure that the seasoning is well incorporated and evenly distributed on each bok choy leaf.

Serve immediately or allow to ferment, covered, at room temperature, for 1 day. If not eating right away, refrigerate and consume within 3 days.

Stuffed Cucumber Kimchi

Oi Sobagi (TRADITIONAL)

Indigenous Korean cucumbers—which are delicate, a tender pea-pod green, and have few seeds—resemble large Israeli cucumbers or Japanese and English slicing cucumbers more than standard hothouse cucumbers. Kirby or Persian cucumbers, which are widely available, make a great substitute—they have a thinner skin and few seeds, unlike American hothouse cucumbers, which have a thick skin and large seeds.

The cucumbers in this classic summer kimchi recipe are served stuffed. Some like to add a bit of garlic, but my mom says that the chives are pungent enough. These stuffed cucumbers are ubiquitous in the summer and served alongside several dishes that often accompany most Korean meals; they're not quite a condiment, and not quite a snack, but are always present at the table, complementing the main course.

In this kimchi, the flavors of the cucumbers are highlighted by the subtle bite from the chives. If you can't find Korean chives (see page 21), you can substitute regular green onions instead. I love the contrasting colors of this summer staple—the vibrant green of the cucumbers and the red of the chile peppers. This is a very popular kimchi, especially with children who are trying kimchi for the first time and might be timid; you can adjust the amount of chile peppers to suit your family's palate. The stuffed cucumbers release a lot of juice during fermentation, and that delicious spicy pickle juice is a great addition to cold rice noodle soup

> Prep: 50 minutes   > Brine: 30 minutes   > Fermentation: 1 to 2 days   > Makes 6 cups (4 to 6 servings)

Brine

2 pounds cucumbers, unpeeled but ends trimmed (about 8 Kirby, 10 Persian, or 2 large English cucumbers)

2 tablespoons kosher salt

Stuffing

1/4 cup Korean chile pepper flakes

6 ounces Korean chives, finely chopped, or 8 green onions, green and white parts, finely chopped (about 1 cup)

1/2 cup shredded carrot (about 1 carrot; optional)

1 teaspoon sugar

Cut the cucumbers in half widthwise and make a deep X-shaped incision extending two-thirds of the way down the inside of each cucumber. Place the cucumbers in a sieve set over a bowl, sprinkle with the salt, and set aside for 30 minutes to drain. For an even cure, make sure to rub salt inside each incision. Reserve the drained liquid.

To make the stuffing, in a medium bowl, combine the chile pepper flakes, chives, carrot, and sugar. Add 3 tablespoons of water to form a thin paste, and set aside for 5 minutes to let the flavors combine.

CONTINUED

Rinse the salt off the cucumbers and pat them dry. Using a teaspoon, stuff the chile pepper flake mixture into the cucumbers (a grapefruit spoon, with its pointy ridges, also works well here), being careful to place the stuffing into all the cucumbers' crevices. Do two passes: the first focusing on the horizontal segments, the second on the vertical.

Place the cucumbers in 2 quart-size containers or 3 wide-mouth pint jars and spoon the remaining stuffing on top. Pour the reserved brining liquid into the containers, cover, and set aside at room temperature, for 1 to 2 days depending on the ambient temperature. (Between 65°F and 70°F is ideal.) If the temperature of your room is too warm or humid, consider fermenting at room temperature for only 1 day, then moving the stuffed cucumbers to the refrigerator to finish fermenting; keep in mind that the fermentation process in the refrigerator is slower, so the total time will likely be 3 to 4 days. Check for crunchiness and balance of flavors—you should be tasting the salty, the sweet, and the savory. Serve the cucumbers when they've reached a level of crunchiness that you like. Leftovers can be refrigerated for 3 to 7 days.

NOTE

Cucumbers tend to get soggy and limp over time, but the flavors will continue to develop. Ideally you want to consume these cucumbers within 3 to 7 days. Reserve the delicious kimchi pickle juice to serve with rice noodles for a refreshing summer meal, or use as a cold soup.

Quick Cucumber and Chive Kimchi

Oi Buchu Gutjori (TRADITIONAL)

The beauty of this kimchi, celebrating the marriage of crispy, fresh cucumber and piquant spices, is in its immediacy. Requiring no fermentation time, this kimchi can be eaten instantly. This traditional dish is a perfect complement to a main course such as grilled fish, roasted chicken, or topped on salads. If you can't find Korean chives (see page 21), use green onions or European chives. The anchovy sauce is optional—use it if you want an extra kick of flavor.

› Prep: 20 minutes   › Brine: 5 to 7 minutes   › Fermentation: Ready to eat   › Makes 5 cups (6 to 8 servings)

2 pounds cucumbers, unpeeled (about 8 to
  10 Kirby, 10 Persian, or 2 large Japanese
  or slicing greenhouse cucumbers)
2 tablespoons kosher salt
2 tablespoons Korean chile pepper flakes
2 teaspoons anchovy sauce (optional)
1¹/₂ teaspoons sugar
3 ounces Korean chives, or 4 green onions,
  green part only, cut into thin diagonal slivers
  (about ¹/₄ cup)
2 tablespoons thinly sliced onion

Halve the cucumbers lengthwise, then cut them into ¹/₄-inch diagonal slices. In a medium bowl, mix the cucumbers with the salt until well combined. Set aside for 5 to 7 minutes, until the cucumbers sweat and glisten. They will lose some firmness, but should still have a little crunch.

Place the cucumbers in a colander and rinse, then pat them dry. In a medium bowl, combine the cucumbers with the chile pepper flakes, anchovy sauce, and sugar and set aside for 10 minutes to let the flavors combine. Add the chives and onion and toss to combine.

Eat immediately, or refrigerate and consume within 2 to 3 days.

FARMERS' MARKET TIP

Try adding thin slices of watermelon radish from your local farmers' market to this kimchi recipe or to liquid-type kimchi recipes such as Tri-Colored Bell Pepper and Cabbage Water Kimchi in Clear Broth (page 42). They are a visually appealing and refreshing addition to summer kimchi recipes such as these two.

Tri-Colored Bell Pepper and Cabbage Water Kimchi in Clear Broth

Nabak Yang Kochu Mulkimchi (CONTEMPORARY)

This is another cool, refreshing, traditional take on the cold, water-based soup kimchi. But unlike some mulkimchi (see opposite), this dish uses colorful bell peppers in a clear broth and no chile peppers. Visually it's a feast for the eyes. (Note that the peppers may discolor as they ferment; their colors will be brightest in the first few days.) The result is a tangy pickling broth that is effervescent and savory. If you have sea salt on hand, try using it for a slightly brinier finish, which is nice in the summer, though kosher salt will also work. This clear broth complements the vegetables' crisp notes and is delicious served alongside tangy barbecue, curry dishes, or spicy Mexican food. Add some cooked rice noodles to this dish to make a pleasant summer dinner.

› Prep: 1 hour › Brine: 45 minutes › Fermentation: 1 to 2 days › Makes 12 cups (6 to 8 servings)

2 tablespoons kosher salt, or 2¹/2 to 3 tablespoons sea salt

2 cups water

1 pound (about ¹/2 head) Savoy or green cabbage, cut into nabak shape (see page 22; 4 cups)

1 bunch table radishes, halved (about 2 cups)

¹/4 cup sliced yellow onion

2 green onions, green and white parts, cut into 2-inch pieces (about ¹/3 cup)

1 tablespoon minced garlic

1 teaspoon peeled, grated fresh ginger

1 teaspoon sugar

¹/2 red bell pepper, seeded, cut into nabak shape (see page 22; about ²/3 cup)

¹/2 yellow bell pepper, seeded, cut into nabak shape (see page 22; about ²/3 cup)

¹/2 green bell pepper, seeded, cut into nabak shape (see page 22; about ²/3 cup)

In a large bowl, combine the salt with the water. Add the cabbage and radishes and set aside for 45 minutes. Strain the cabbage and set aside; reserve the brining liquid.

In a large bowl, combine the onions, garlic, ginger, and sugar with 4 cups water, and stir to dissolve. Add the brined cabbage and radishes with the bell peppers, the onion mixture, and the reserved brining liquid. Transfer to a 3-quart container, cover, and allow to ferment at room temperature for up to 2 days. You will note tiny bubbles forming in the liquid after one or two days, which is a sign of fermentation. Refrigerate and eat within 1 week.

Korean "Gazpacho" Water Kimchi in Red Pepper Broth

Nabak Baechu Mulkimchi (TRADITIONAL)

Mulkimchi means "water kimchi"—a saturated red broth laced with Korean chile pepper flakes (*gochugaru*). It's a refreshing, cold soup with a bracing bite, made with napa cabbage and daikon radish that is cut into precise squares, *nabak*-style. In Korean, *nabak* means "cut into thin flat squares," usually about 1½-inch squares that are ⅛ inch thick, a traditional shape for daikon radishes used throughout kimchi making. The uniform size and shape of the bite-size vegetables, as well as their thin, flat surface, allows them to brine quickly and evenly and makes for a stunning presentation.

Many summer kimchi recipes are based on the idea of a cold, refreshing pickled soup. This kimchi's flavors remind me of gazpacho, Spain's celebrated cold, summertime tomato soup from the Andalusia region. Nabak Baechu Mulkimchi is a chilled, mildly spicy soup with a tangy broth redolent of peppers and garlic and is pure savory refreshment. But whereas gazpacho's acidity stems from sherry vinegar, the acidity in this dish comes from natural fermentation.

To make this soup into a full summer meal that requires virtually no cooking, add some cold rice or vermicelli noodles (as pictured on page 45). Or eat it as is—it's a perfect way to whet the appetite. The traditional recipe calls for daikon radishes. However, regular table radishes will work fine as a substitute; just keep in mind that regular radishes tend to get soggy sooner, and so must be consumed faster. And although mulkimchi is most refreshing in the summer, you can make it year-round with a variety of vegetables. Experiment by adding hardy fruits such as apples, pears, or even persimmons in the fall for a more contemporary twist.

› Prep: 40 minutes › Brine: 20 minutes › Fermentation: 1 to 2 days › Makes 12 cups (6 to 8 servings)

¾ pound young, summer napa cabbage, cut into nabak shape (see page 22; about 4 cups)

1 pound daikon radish, trimmed and cut into nabak shape (see page 22; about 3 cups); or table radishes sliced ⅛ inch thick

2 tablespoons kosher salt

2 tablespoons Korean chile pepper flakes

4 green onions, green part only, diagonally cut in thin slivers (about ¼ cup)

1 cup thinly sliced yellow onion

3 carrots, diagonally cut ¼ inch thick (about 1 cup; optional)

1 Holland Red pepper, sliced thinly diagonally, with seeds removed (optional)

1 cup Sweet Rice-Flour Porridge (page 24)

1 tablespoon minced garlic

1 teaspoon peeled, grated fresh ginger

CONTINUED

In a large bowl, mix together the cabbage, radish, and salt and let stand at room temperature for 20 minutes.

In a medium bowl, mix 6 cups water with the chile pepper flakes and allow the flakes to steep in the water for 20 minutes. Using a fine-mesh strainer or two layers of cheesecloth, strain the chile pepper flake broth into another bowl; the broth should not have any chile pepper flakes in it and should have a crimson tint.

In a large bowl, combine the brined cabbage and radish (along with their liquid) with the green onions, yellow onion, carrots, and pepper. Stir in the porridge, garlic, and ginger. Transfer the cabbage mixture and the chile water to a gallon-size container or two 2-quart containers. Cover and let sit at room temperature for 1 to 2 days, then refrigerate and eat within 2 weeks.

Tender Young Napa Cabbage Kimchi

Putbaechu Kimchi (TRADITIONAL)

One of the best ways to enjoy this spring-only crop is in this mildly flavored dish, which is my favorite summertime use of napa cabbage. *Putbaechu*, or "tender cabbage," is the season's first cabbage, which is very tender and delicate. Though it is found mostly in Korean markets, *putbaechu* is worth seeking out. The size of young napa cabbage is closer to bok choy, but it has a completely different flavor. Young napa cabbages are short, with slender, long leaves, and are more reminiscent of romaine lettuce than of cabbage. If you can't find young napa cabbage, substitute Asian mustard greens. The seasonings in the dish complement the watery content of the cabbage and create a refreshing flavor. Fermentation turns the brining liquid of this kimchi into a cold and refreshing, mildly spicy, and tangy broth.

› Prep: 50 minutes › Brine: 30 minutes › Fermentation: 1 to 2 days › Makes 4 cups (4 to 6 servings)

6 to 8 heads (about 1 pound total) young, early
   summer napa cabbage
2 tablespoons kosher salt
1/4 cup Korean chile pepper flakes
2 tablespoons anchovy sauce
1 tablespoon Sweet Rice-Flour Porridge (page 24)
1 teaspoon minced garlic
1 teaspoon sugar

Trim the ends of the cabbage and rinse the leaves thoroughly in a large bowl of water. This vegetable tends to be gritty, so you may have to use several changes of water—I recommend rinsing at least 3 times.

Cut the leaves into strips that are about 4 inches long by 1 inch wide and place them in a large bowl. Toss the leaves with the salt, making sure they are evenly coated; let stand at room temperature for about 30 minutes. Drain the liquid from the bowl, rinse any excess salt off the leaves with cold water, and dry the leaves.

In a large bowl, toss the brined, drained cabbage with the chile pepper flakes, anchovy sauce, porridge, garlic, and sugar until well combined. Place the cabbage mixture in a quart-size jar, cover, and allow to sit at room temperature for 1 to 2 days. Store refrigerated; the kimchi will keep for up to 1 month.

Korean Radish Top Kimchi

Yeolmu Kimchi (TRADITIONAL)

A summertime favorite, *yeolmu* (young summer radish) is a Korean version of table radishes. In Korea, cooks use not only the root of radishes in cooking but also the greens. Due to the diminutive size of these radishes (they resemble tiny tendrils), this kimchi is mostly the tops of the radishes—you'll understand how refreshing and vibrant radish tops can be. *Yeolmu* can be found at Korean markets, and are worth seeking out. You may also substitute round white Hailstone radishes, which are available at farmers' markets during spring and fall. When selecting radish tops, ensure that they are firm but not too thick or spiny textured; try to find the most tender radish tops. Also try using the long radish stems from baby daikon types available at farmers' markets.

I find these radish greens, prepared in a spicy brine, to be a refreshing, chilled summer soup—particularly wonderful on a humid day when the mere idea of turning on your stove makes you break out in a sweat. The cold brine with the crisp radish greens reminds me of the flavors of a Bloody Mary, and the crunchy texture of the greens is reminiscent of celery stick garnish.

› Prep: **1 hour** › Brine: **40 minutes** › Fermentation: **2 days** › Makes 4 cups (6 to 8 servings)

Brine
2 bunches (about 1^1/$_2$ pounds) Korean yeolmu radishes or white hailstone radishes with their tops, wilting and yellow leaves trimmed
^{2}/$_3$ cup kosher salt

Seasoning Paste
2 tablespoons Korean chile pepper flakes
1 tablespoon minced garlic
^{1}/$_2$ tablespoon peeled, grated fresh ginger
3 tablespoons anchovy sauce or Mushroom Broth (page 26)
1 cup Sweet Rice-Flour Porridge (page 24)
1 teaspoon sugar

1 small yellow onion, thinly sliced in semicircles
6 green onions, green parts only, halved lengthwise, then cut into 3-inch pieces (about ^{2}/$_3$ cup)

In a large bowl, thoroughly wash the radishes using 3 to 4 changes of water. Drain in a large colander. Cut the radishes so that the greens are about 3 inches long. You will wind up with some greens still attached to the radishes and some greens alone. Don't worry if some of the greens break off the radish while you're handling them. Cut the radish root (leaving the greens attached, if there are any attached) into quarters.

In a large bowl, combine the radishes and the greens with the salt and set aside for 40 minutes. Drain and reserve ^{1}/$_2$ cup of the brine that accumulates at the bottom. Under running water, rinse the salt off the radishes and the greens and set aside in a colander to drain for at least 10 minutes.

To make the seasoning paste, in a mini food processor fitted with a metal blade, pulse the chile flakes, garlic, ginger, and anchovy sauce into a paste. With the motor running, pour in the porridge and add the sugar. The texture of the mixture should resemble hummus.

In a large bowl, toss the radishes and greens with the onions, then add the seasoning paste and toss until the vegetables are well coated. If the mixture doesn't taste very salty, add a bit of the reserved brine. Transfer to a 2-quart container, cover with a lid, and let sit at room temperature for 2 days. The radishes will taste briny and slightly carbonated. Refrigerate and consume within 1 month.

› Clockwise, from bottom: (A) hailstone radish (aka Tokyo turnip), (B) Korean bachelor radish (*choggak*), (C) table radishes, (D) Korean summer radishes (*yeolmu*), (E) turnip, (F) French breakfast radishes

French Breakfast Radish Kimchi

(CONTEMPORARY)

If you have access to French Breakfast radishes, the farmers' market favorites are ideal for this recipe. They're delicate but denser than regular table radishes. (However, table radishes work just fine, too.) This is a perfect example of how a radish can reveal its delicate summer flavor through proper and complementary seasoning. Try using the entire radish with its top, which may give you a new appreciation for radish flavor—you may never throw out the greens again! Using this kimchi in a summer corn salad (page 104) makes for a new summertime classic.

› Prep: 1 hour › Brine: 20 minutes › Fermentation: 1 day › Makes 4 cups (4 to 6 servings)

Brine
1¹/₂ to 2 pounds French Breakfast radishes or table radishes, with their stems on (stems optional)
1¹/₂ tablespoons kosher salt

Seasoning Paste
¹/₄ cup Mushroom Broth (page 26) or water
2 tablespoons Korean chile pepper flakes
1 teaspoon peeled, finely grated fresh ginger
¹/₂ teaspoon minced garlic
¹/₂ teaspoon sugar

In a large bowl, thoroughly wash the radishes in 3 to 4 changes of water. Drain. Trim any unsightly ends and tops and cut the radishes in half. In another large bowl, toss the radishes with the salt. Let stand for 20 minutes.

To make the seasoning paste, in a small bowl, combine the broth, chile pepper flakes, ginger, garlic, and sugar. Set aside.

Drain the radishes in a colander set over a bowl, reserving the brined juice. Rinse any excess salt off the radishes and let drain for another 15 minutes.

In a large bowl, combine the radishes with the seasoning paste and toss until evenly coated. Pack the radishes into a quart-size jar. Pour the reserved brining liquid into the bowl that was used to coat the radishes with the seasonings, and swirl the liquid around to capture any leftover seasonings. Pour into the jar, cover with a lid, and let sit at room temperature for 1 day. Refrigerate and consume within 1 week.

The Kimchi Cookbook

Perilla Leaf Kimchi

Kaennip Kimchi (TRADITIONAL)

Perilla leaf, a relative of shiso, has a faint citrus-mint flavor, and is a treasured summertime treat in Korea. These delicate leaves look like large mint leaves and are layered together into a large stack. While perilla leaves aren't easy to find (they're usually available at Korean markets), tracking them down for this kimchi is well worth the effort. If you substitute shiso leaf, bear in mind that the results will be different, as shiso tends to be more potent and fragrant. Although Perilla Leaf Kimchi ferments in a stack, the leaves are eaten individually. It is often enjoyed as a wrap or eaten alongside rice; try it with grilled chicken or beef for a quick *ssam* wrap (a vegetable leaf enclosing a stuffing, usually meat and rice). Or for a minty, spicy twist, try this flavorful kimchi in a grilled chicken sandwich with mayo.

› Prep: 1 hour › Brine: 30 minutes › Fermentation: 6 hours to 1 day
› Makes one 40-piece stack (4 to 6 servings)

Brine
30 to 40 leaves (about 3 ounces) young perilla
   leaves, including stems
2 tablespoons kosher salt

Seasoning Paste
1/4 cup Sweet Rice-Flour Porridge (page 24)
2 tablespoons anchovy sauce
2 tablespoons Korean chile pepper flakes
2 teaspoons minced garlic
1 teaspoon peeled, minced fresh ginger
1 tablespoon chile pepper threads, optional

In a large bowl, combine the perilla leaves and salt and just enough water to cover the leaves. Let stand for 30 minutes and then drain.

To make the seasoning paste, in a small bowl, stir together the porridge, anchovy sauce, chili pepper flakes, garlic, ginger, and chile pepper threads (see page 17).

Spoon about 1 teaspoon of the seasoning paste onto the center of a perilla leaf, spreading the paste to the outer edges to get an even coating. Repeat this step on a second leaf, and place the second leaf on top of the first. Continue with the remaining leaves, until you have a stack of leaves. When finished, place the stack in a resealable plastic bag, flat container, or on a plate. If using a bag, remove any air pockets and seal tightly against the leaves. If in a container or on a plate, cover the leaves with plastic wrap placed directly over the top leaves to ensure that there is no contact with oxygen. Let stand at room temperature for 6 hours and up to 1 day for more developed flavors. Refrigerate and consume within 1 month.

Chive Kimchi

Buchu Kimchi (TRADITIONAL)

Korean chives, or *buchu*, look like long, flat blades of grass and appear in numerous Korean dishes. Korean chives have a more substantial appearance than thin, delicate European chives, and have subtle garlic notes. Korean chives can be found in Korean markets; the Chinese variety tends to be more readily available and makes for a fine substitute, although it is a bit longer and firmer than the shorter, more delicate *buchu*. The flavor of this recipe will vary depending on the chives you use, but the result will be a punchy kimchi-without-borders, with flavors that continue to evolve as it ages. Consider adding some to a rice bowl, a chicken wrap, or a few strands topped on your salad for an extra kick.

› Prep: 20 minutes › Fermentation: 2 days › Makes about 1 cup (6 to 8 servings)

6 ounces Korean chives or 1 bunch European chives, ends trimmed, yellow and wilted parts discarded, and sliced into 4- to 6-inch strips (about 1 cup)

1 tablespoon Korean chile pepper flakes

2 tablespoons anchovy sauce or Mushroom Broth (page 26)

In a large bowl, combine the chives with the chile pepper flakes and the anchovy sauce, and toss to evenly coat the chives. Place in a $^{1}/_{2}$-pint jar or resealable plastic bag, and remove as much air as possible. Seal tightly, and allow to sit at room temperature for 2 days. Refrigerate and use within 2 months.

Green Onion Kimchi

Paa Kimchi (TRADITIONAL)

Green onions can be found everywhere—from farmers' markets to grocery stores. Try to buy early spring green onions from a farmer—young onions have a slightly curved, more bulbous head; long, beautiful green stems; and a brighter, more tender flavor than supermarket green onions. Garlic scapes could also work well as an alternative. Traditionally, green onions are kept intact for this kimchi.

This kimchi has a strong green onion flavor but imparts a spicy, tanginess as it ages—it is mostly used as a condiment. A little goes a long way, as the spicy green onion flavor adds an unexpected touch to dishes. Try Green Onion Kimchi as an ingredient in savory Kimchi Cornmeal Pancakes (page 106) and Kimchi Frittata with Green Onions and Shiitakes (page 102).

> Prep: 40 minutes > Brine: 20 minutes > Fermentation: Ready to eat or overnight, depending on your preference > Makes 3 cups (8 to 12 servings)

1/2 pound green onions, spring onions, or garlic scapes
1/2 tablespoon kosher salt
2 tablespoons Korean chile pepper flakes
1/2 tablespoon sugar
1 tablespoon anchovy sauce

In a large bowl, combine the onions with the salt and let sit at room temperature for 20 minutes. Drain and discard the liquid.

In another large bowl, stir together the chile pepper flakes, sugar, and anchovy sauce.

Add the brined onions to the pepper-flake mixture and combine well. Let the onions marinate, uncovered, for 20 minutes before serving. Or let them marinate overnight, covered, at room temperature for more pungent flavors.

Refrigerate and consume within 1 month. Notice the changes in taste as the flavors develop further into tangy notes.

Cipollini Onion Kimchi

Yangpaa Kimchi (CONTEMPORARY)

These cipollini onions are a great accompaniment to roasted Brussels sprouts (page 117), or use them as a salad topping. If you can't find cipollini onions, use another type of small, mild-tasting onion, such as first-of-spring small onions, if available. You can substitute pearl onions for cipollinis, but their diminutive size might make them cumbersome to peel and cut. Should you want to try pearl onions, use fresh ones, as frozen pearl onions have a texture that won't work well in the recipe. Because the flavors of this kimchi are so strong, you will probably use this sparingly and only as a condiment. But cooking the onions will release the natural sweetness that occurs during caramelization—you can toss this kimchi in with other root vegetables the next time you roast a chicken.

› Prep: 1 hour › Brine: 30 minutes › Fermentation: 1 to 2 days › Makes 2 cups (8 to 12 servings)

Brine
12 ounces cipollini onions or pearl onions, trimmed, peeled, and quartered (about 14 onions)
2 teaspoons kosher salt

Seasoning Paste
2 tablespoons Korean chile pepper flakes
2 tablespoons anchovy sauce or Mushroom Broth (page 26)
1 teaspoon sugar
3 tablespoons coarsely shredded carrot (about 1 medium carrot)
1 tablespoon Sweet Rice-Flour Porridge (page 24)

In a medium bowl, toss the onions with the salt and set aside for 30 minutes. Rinse and drain the onions.

To make the seasoning paste, in a large bowl, combine the chile pepper flakes, anchovy sauce, sugar, and carrot. Set aside the spice paste for 10 minutes to let the flavors combine before stirring in the porridge.

Add the onions to the spice paste and toss until well combined. Transfer the onions to a glass pint jar with a tight-fitting lid and let the onions ferment, covered, at room temperature, for 1 to 2 days. Refrigerate and consume within 2 weeks.

Deconstructed "Stuffed" Eggplant Kimchi

Kagi Sobagi Kimchi (CONTEMPORARY)

For this recipe, you can use Japanese eggplant or Italian eggplant (preferably small ones)—both work well here. This is a contemporary version of the traditional *sobagi* method of stuffing an eggplant with a seasoning mixture. It's much like stuffed cucumbers (page 37) but with delicate fleshy flavors of fresh eggplant and spice notes. I prefer this deconstructed version, as it is easier to make, and cutting the eggplant into pieces exposes more flesh to the seasonings, which intensifies the flavors. The eggplant and other vegetables, tossed with the spicy seasoning paste, make an excellent complement to salads, grilled chicken, or sandwiches. Try it alongside a plate of fresh mozzarella, or put a new twist on an eggplant Parmesan sandwich, and you'll be hooked on these Korean-spiced eggplant flavors.

›Prep: 1 hour ›Brine: 30 minutes ›Fermentation: 1 day ›Makes about 4 cups (4 to 6 servings)

Brine
1¹/₂ to 2 pounds Japanese eggplant (about 2 to 3) or Italian eggplant (about 1 to 2)
2 tablespoons kosher salt

Seasoning Paste
2 tablespoons Korean chile pepper flakes
1 tablespoon anchovy sauce
1 teaspoon minced garlic
¹/₂ teaspoon peeled, grated fresh ginger

²/₃ cup thinly sliced red onion
²/₃ cup thinly sliced red bell pepper (about ¹/₂ bell pepper)
¹/₄ cup finely chopped Korean chives or green onions, green part only

Trim the ends of each eggplant and halve the eggplant widthwise. Slice each eggplant half into quarters lengthwise. In a large bowl, toss the eggplant with the salt, rubbing the salt into the fleshy parts of the eggplant. Let sit for 30 minutes.

To make the seasoning paste, in a small bowl, combine the chile pepper flakes, anchovy sauce, garlic, and ginger. While the eggplant brines, let the mixture rest so the flavors combine.

Once the eggplant is brined, add the onion, bell pepper, and chives to the bowl. Add the seasoning paste and toss well so that the paste is evenly distributed. Refrigerate immediately and allow the flavors to develop overnight. Consume within 5 to 7 days. Keep refrigerated.

Stuffed Tomato Kimchi

Tomato Sobagi (CONTEMPORARY)

Tomatoes are excellent at taking on flavors and absorbing a brine. While this isn't a traditional kimchi recipe, tomatoes, with their bright acidity and savory flavors, are a perfect complement to the kimchi spices. Use vine-ripened red or green tomatoes, if you can find them—the fermentation and acidity will ripen with the tomatoes and create a delicious, bold flavor. The stuffed tomatoes can be eaten immediately or, if you want a more pronounced, deeper flavor, can ferment for up to two days. They're the perfect accompaniment to fried chicken and corn on the cob, or serve them with a bit of fresh ricotta cheese as an appetizer.

› Prep: 30 minutes › Brine: 15 to 20 minutes › Fermentation: Ready to eat, or 1 day, depending on your preference › Makes 4 stuffed tomatoes

Brine

4 medium tomatoes on the vine (about 1¹/₂ to 2 pounds)

1¹/₂ teaspoons kosher salt

Seasoning Paste

¹/₄ cup Korean chile pepper flakes

2 teaspoons sugar

2 tablespoons anchovy sauce or Mushroom Broth (page 26)

2 teaspoons finely minced garlic

¹/₂ cup coarsely grated daikon radish (about ¹/₃ medium)

¹/₂ cup minced Korean or European chives

3 green onions, green and white parts, julienned (about ¹/₂ cup)

Using a paring knife, make an X-shaped incision in the bottom (not the stem side) of each tomato, cutting two-thirds of the way down. Rub the insides with the salt and set aside for 15 to 20 minutes.

To make the seasoning paste, in a large bowl, mix together the chile pepper flakes, sugar, anchovy sauce, and garlic. Set aside for 10 minutes to let the flavors combine.

Add the radish, chives, and onions to the bowl with the seasoning paste and toss until thoroughly coated.

Stuff each tomato with the seasoned radish mixture, layer any excess stuffing on top of the tomatoes, and set aside for 30 minutes before serving or allow to ferment, covered, at room temperature, for 1 day. Refrigerate and consume within 2 days.

FALL / WINTER KIMCHI

The arrival of fall signals harvest time in Korea, and one of the most famous fall events is *kimjang*, the renowned cabbage harvest, which is followed by kimchi making. Think of it as the Korean equivalent of "putting up" summer fruits and vegetables in the American canning tradition. As a historically agrarian culture, Koreans have a deep reverence for their land. Due to Korea's long, cold winters, and before the advent of refrigeration, *kimjang* was an important annual rite marking fall's transition to winter. Making kimchi was the only means of preserving the harvest vegetables, along with their nutrients, for the frigid months ahead. Today, fewer people participate in *kimjang* (because napa cabbage is now readily available year-round), but it remains an important part of the cultural significance of kimchi.

Unlike the flavors of spring/summer kimchi, which require little fermentation and result in a lighter touch on the palate, the flavors of cold-weather kimchi are bold and complex. They're the result of a longer fermentation time—anywhere from just a few days to several months. Keeping the vegetables whole or cut into halves, plus using an overnight saltwater brine, also brings out a deeper flavor in the kimchi. In addition, the initial brining stage for fall/winter kimchi varies anywhere from a few hours to overnight versus a quick 15- to 30-minute dry-salt brine for summer kimchi.

Kimjang is one of my earliest childhood memories involving food. I recall watching my grandmother participate in an elaborate process of brining, stuffing, and stacking cabbage halves into the big earthenware jars (*onggi*) that she kept in her backyard. The event, which brings together neighbors and relatives (imagine a kimchi-making block party), usually involves several households that, over the course of a few days, make enough kimchi to last for several months. I am told that an average of about 150 pounds (40 to 50 cabbage heads) of kimchi per family was made each fall. Prior to refrigeration (and kimchi refrigerators) and the premade kimchi industry, making your own batch of kimchi was the only way to ensure that you had an ample supply of vegetables to last you through the winter.

Kimjang is mostly focused on *poggi* kimchi—napa cabbage halves that are seasoned and stuffed with a spicy filling. There must have been at least 500 pounds of napa cabbage kimchi, halved and stuffed with a seasoning paste, at my grandmother's house. I remember that a whole day was dedicated to the process of brining and rinsing. The next day would be spent solely on stuffing the cabbage halves. The seasoned filling was carefully spread between each of the leaves and tightly packed inside the earthenware jars. Each household would have several vessels in their backyard. Storing the *onggi* underground at a cool temperature (between 45°F and 55°F), ensured a slow, steady fermentation in a dark, cave-like environment similar to a cheese or wine cave in Western Europe. The *onggi* was buried underground and straw mats that were placed on top of the lids, which acted as a protective layer to keep the kimchi from freezing. The earthenware jar's advantage is that being made out of clay, it has micropores that allow the kimchi to breathe, all the while retaining liquid and sealing it off from most oxygen and light.

Another popular winter kimchi is fermented daikon radish, or *dongchimi* (page 95), which uses a liquid brine and is prized for its crisp taste. Keeping vegetables in whole or halved pieces allows for a slow fermentation, which brings out their natural bracing acidity and tanginess. It is precisely because chile pepper flakes are absent from this kimchi that it makes such a refreshing accompaniment to winter dishes like spicy stews and soups that are served tableside piping hot. Bachelor Radish Kimchi (page 87) is another very popular kimchi typically eaten during the winter months. The crunch of these miniature daikon radishes, with their long stems, highlights a delicious contrast of textures of both the greens and the radishes.

Wrapped kimchi (pages 73 and 76) hails from an age-old culinary tradition. *Bossam* translates loosely into "wrapping the stuffing." It is not a common kimchi—it's made only on special occasions—but the idea of wrapping precious delicacies in the leaves of napa cabbage is an important one in Korea. The rolled-up kimchi is a playful nod to this wrapping idea, but it uses regular cabbage, which is more readily available.

Vegetables used in winter kimchis are typically fermented in large or whole pieces, which is ideal for both root vegetables and cabbage halves. The spice and kimchi flavors become more pungent because the fermentation process is kept at a steady pace in a cool environment. Be sure to get a feel for the range of winter kimchi, from *mak* kimchi to whole stuffed kimchi. As you become more comfortable making winter kimchi, make double batches so that you can test out different fermentation stages. Make more for long-term aging to see how flavors develop, as these are the anchors of kimchi making. These kimchis will be invaluable to you as ingredients in the final section of this book (pages 97–141), which is dedicated to cooking with kimchi. You'll be glad you made extra batches, as the depth of flavor can't be hurried and the special flavor notes and acidity are only achieved by long-term fermentation. Winter's vegetables do not have to be bland any more; instead they can be a celebration of kimchi's bold and spicy seasonings. Think about creating your family's own *kimjang* tradition to add some vibrancy to your winter vegetables.

Instant Apple, Persimmon, and Pear Kimchi

Sagyua, Gaam, Bae Kimchi (TRADITIONAL)

This trio of fruit plays on the idea of combining the sweet, the savory, and the spicy by using apples, persimmons, and pears—celebrated autumnal fruits in Korea. Choose young, firm Fuyu persimmons and crisp, juicy Asian pears for their bright flavors. And, building on the Korean tradition of using radish stems, incorporating often-discarded parsley stems here gives the fruit mixture a refreshingly potent parsley flavor that complements the fruity-spice flavors nicely. Serve this kimchi as you would a chutney with a chicken sandwich, roasted turkey, or baked ham.

› Prep: 15 minutes › Fermentation: Ready to eat › Makes 3 cups (4 servings)

1 pound Fuyu persimmons (about 4 small or 2 medium), peeled, cored, quartered, and cut into 1/8-inch-thick slices

1/2 Asian or Bosc pear, peeled, cored, quartered, and cut into 1/8-inch-thick slices

1 medium apple (such as Fuji, Gala, or Honeycrisp), peeled, cored, quartered, and cut into 1/8-inch-thick slices

12 stems flat-leaf parsley, cut into 1 1/2-inch pieces

1 teaspoon Korean chile pepper flakes

1/2 teaspoon chopped garlic

1/2 teaspoon anchovy sauce

In a small mixing bowl, combine the persimmons, pear, apple, and parsley. Add the chile pepper flakes, garlic, and anchovy sauce and mix until well combined. Let stand for 15 minutes for the flavors to blend. Serve immediately or refrigerate, covered, and consume within 2 days.

Apple, Pear, and Cabbage Water Kimchi with Fennel in Clear Broth

Nabak Sagyua, Bae, Baechu Mulkimchi (CONTEMPORARY)

Think of this as a first-of-fall kimchi recipe, one to make when you know that summer has slipped away, but before the weather becomes cold. There is less daylight, the nights are longer and cooler, and there's an autumnal crispness to the air.

This near-instant water kimchi is a transitional recipe for your kimchi-making repertoire, requiring no more than half a day of fermentation; it is best served chilled, perhaps for lunch on a still somewhat warm afternoon. The apples and pears, combined with the cabbage and celery, offer delightful crunch and texture. Shaved fennel offers subtle notes of licorice with a hint of sweetness that works well with the fruit. All together, this cold, refreshing, soup-like kimchi is the perfect prelude to fall, when it's still warm out, but the oppressiveness of summer's heat is long gone.

› Prep: 30 minutes › Brine: 30 minutes › Fermentation: **Ready to eat** › Makes 8 cups (4 to 6 servings)

1/2 head (about 1 pound) napa cabbage or green cabbage, cut into nabak shape (see page 22; about 4 cups)

2 tablespoons kosher salt

1 medium Asian pear

1 medium apple (preferably Cortland, Fuji, or another firm variety)

1/4 medium yellow onion

1 tablespoon minced garlic

1 tablespoon peeled, finely grated fresh ginger

2 teaspoons sugar

4 cups cold water

1 medium fennel bulb, thinly shaved

In a large bowl, mix together the cabbage and the salt. Let stand for 30 minutes.

Meanwhile, peel, core, and quarter the Asian pear and the apple. Cut the fruit into 1/4-inch-thick slices.

In a mini food processor fitted with a metal blade, puree together the onion, garlic, and ginger. Transfer the pureed mixture to a large bowl, add the sugar and the water, and stir well. Add the cabbage, along with its brine, the apple, pear, and fennel and mix well. Serve immediately, or refrigerate, covered, and consume within 1 month.

Cauliflower Water Kimchi with Pear, Lime Zest, and Pomegranate in Clear Broth

Cauliflower Sukryu Mulkimchi (CONTEMPORARY)

While thinking of pickled vegetables in an Italian antipasti course, I was inspired to make a *mulkimchi* using cauliflower, one of my favorite vegetables and a winter underdog. The flavors of lime, cauliflower, and pomegranate make this a delicate and visually stunning treat, which is perfect for serving on your next antipasti plate or with charcuterie. This recipe is very open to experimentation—consider adding some fennel slices or celery to add more crunch and texture. Feel free to reduce the amount of jalapeño, if you prefer less heat.

› Prep: 15 minutes › Brine: 40 minutes › Fermentation: 1 to 2 days › Makes 10 cups (4 to 6 servings)

1 head (about 2 to 2 1/4 pounds) cauliflower, chopped into small florets

2 tablespoons kosher salt, plus more to taste

1/2 cup plus 2 tablespoons pomegranate arils

1 jalapeño pepper, halved, seeded, and thinly sliced

1 Asian pear, peeled, cored, quartered, and sliced into 1/4-inch-thick pieces

3 cups water

2 teaspoons finely grated lime zest (about 1 lime), plus more to taste

2 teaspoons fresh lime juice (about 1/4 lime), plus more to taste

2 teaspoons peeled, finely grated fresh ginger, plus more to taste

1 1/2 teaspoons minced garlic, plus more to taste

1 tablespoon Sweet Rice-Flour Porridge (page 24)

In a large bowl, toss together the cauliflower and the salt and let sit for 40 minutes. Add the pomegranate arils, jalapeño, and pear and gently toss to combine. Add the water and stir in the lime zest, juice, ginger, and garlic. Taste and adjust the seasonings. Stir in the porridge.

Ladle the kimchi into several quart- or pint-size glass jars or plastic containers, cover with lids, and let sit for 1 to 2 days at room temperature. Refrigerate and consume within 2 months.

Butternut Squash Kimchi with Lacinato Kale and Pine Nuts

Hobak Kimchi (CONTEMPORARY)

This beautiful fall kimchi is a contemporary spin on a traditional recipe made during the abundant Korean squash harvest. Inspired by my travels in Italy, I used Lacinato kale and pine nuts, giving this kimchi an Italian flare. Although fermentation is recommended, try eating this kimchi just after it's made, when the flavors are still quite raw and its natural sweetness and crunch shines. As it continues to age, it will develop tangier, more fermented flavors. Brining the squash brings out its natural sweetness, which reminds me of a Fuyu persimmon. Use the Mushroom Broth (page 26) to enhance the earthy flavor. This kimchi goes well with farro salad (page 113) and makes a great side or topping for other grain salads. It may become a staple kimchi all year long; if you can see beyond the hard work of peeling and cutting the squash, you will be rewarded.

› Prep: 20 minutes › Brine: 40 minutes › Fermentation: 2 to 3 days › Makes 4 cups (4 to 6 servings)

1 1/2 pounds butternut squash (about 1/2 of a small squash), peeled, cored, quartered, and cut into 1/8-inch-thick slices

4 1/2 cups water

2 tablespoons kosher salt, plus 2 1/4 teaspoons

2 cups finely chopped Lacinato kale (about 1/2 bunch)

2 tablespoons Korean chile pepper flakes

1 teaspoon chopped garlic

1/2 teaspoon peeled, finely grated fresh ginger

2 tablespoons pine nuts

1/2 cup Mushroom Broth (page 26; optional)

1 teaspoon sugar

In a large bowl, mix the squash with 4 cups of the water and the 2 tablespoons salt. Set aside for 40 minutes. Drain the brine and allow the squash to dry in the colander.

Meanwhile, in a medium colander, toss the kale with 2 teaspoons of the salt and set aside for 15 minutes. Using the colander, rinse off any excess salt with water, then set the colander over a bowl and allow the remaining water to drain into the bowl. Set aside the water that drains off the rinsed kale.

In a large bowl, combine the squash and kale with the chile pepper flakes, garlic, ginger, and pine nuts and toss until the seasonings are well incorporated. Place the mixture into a quart-size container with a tight lid. Swirl the water that drained off the kale and add 1/2 cup water and the remaining 1/4 teaspoon salt. Or, use mushroom broth in place of the water and salt. Add the sugar and stir to dissolve. Ladle the mixture into the container until one-third of the contents are covered.

Allow the mixture to ferment at room temperature for 2 to 3 days. Refrigerate and consume within 1 month.

The Kimchi Cookbook

Rolled-Up Green Cabbage Kimchi with Radish and Asian Pear

Yang Baechu Sobagi Kimchi (CONTEMPORARY)

This style of kimchi builds on the tradition of stuffing the vegetable, but uses green cabbage leaves to create a roll (think dried seaweed in a sushi roll), which is cut into bite-size pieces when you are ready to serve. With properly brined cabbage leaves, you should be able to taste the subtle sweetness and easily fill the leaves with a delicious stuffing—the leaves will act as a showcase for the stuffing.

The sweetness of this common green cabbage, contrasted with the red spicy stuffing, creates a crossroad where East meets West. Serve alongside pork chops or grilled sausages.

Be sure to have a square or rectangular container (at least 8 by 8 inches) with a lid or a gallon-size resealable plastic bag on hand.

› Prep: 1 hour › Brine: 1 to 1¹/₂ hours › Fermentation: 2 to 3 days › Makes 8 rolls (4 to 6 servings)

Brine
³/₄ cup kosher salt
6 cups water
8 large whole outer green cabbage leaves

Seasoning Paste
1 tablespoon sugar
1 tablespoon salted shrimp
2 tablespoons anchovy sauce
1 tablespoon minced garlic
¹/₂ tablespoon peeled, finely grated fresh ginger
¹/₂ cup Korean chile pepper flakes

1 Asian pear, peeled, cored, and julienned
1 cup peeled and julienned turnip (about 2 medium)
    or daikon radish (about ¹/₃ piece of medium)
¹/₄ cup shredded carrot (about 1 small carrot)

In a large bowl, dissolve the salt in 6 cups water and add the cabbage leaves. Use a heavy plate as a weight to fully submerge the cabbage leaves. Let sit for about 1 hour. If, after an hour, the cabbage leaves do not look wilted and limp, allow another 20 minutes of brining time. Continue brining until the leaves are limp, pliable, and translucent. Pay particular attention to the thick parts of the middle white rib of the cabbage; if they are still firm, brine for 10 minutes more. When they're ready, rinse the leaves and pat them dry with a towel. Set aside.

To make the seasoning paste, in a mini food processor fitted with a metal blade, pulse together the sugar, shrimp, anchovy sauce, garlic, and ginger. Add the chile pepper flakes and pulse again to incorporate. The mixture should have the texture of hummus.

CONTINUED

In a medium bowl, combine the seasoning paste, Asian pear, turnip, and carrot.

Place the brined cabbage leaves on a flat surface, and, using a paring knife, trim and remove any thick parts of the central middle white rib of the cabbage. Place 3 tablespoons of stuffing onto each leaf, depending on its size, and roll tightly so that it resembles a sushi roll. Place the rolls tightly next to one another in a square or rectangular container, layering them on top of one another if necessary. Cover tightly with plastic wrap directly over the surface to ensure there is no contact with air, then cover tightly with the lid. Let stand at room temperature for 2 days. The cabbage skins should be translucent and the stuffing flavors well combined. Refrigerate and consume within 2 weeks.

When you're ready to serve the cabbage rolls, slice each roll horizontally into pieces about 1 inch thick, being careful to keep the rolls intact, as if slicing a sushi roll.

MAKE IT VEGAN

Instead of anchovy and shrimp, use 3 tablespoons Mushroom Broth (page 26) to make this recipe vegan-friendly. If you do not want to use sugar or mushroom broth, puree 1/2 peeled apple and add 2 teaspoons sea salt.

White Wrapped Kimchi with Persimmon and Dates

Baek Bossam Kimchi (TRADITIONAL)

This white kimchi is a specialty from Kaesong, just north of Seoul, in what is now North Korea. Kaesong was the old capital of Korea, during the 500-year Koryo Dynasty, and the region is famous for its refined, rich culinary history, and known for this kimchi. The kimchi dates back to before the seventeenth century, before chile peppers were introduced to Korea, and thus is not spicy, but rather crisp and delicate.

The term *bossam* refers to making the *ssam*, or wrapping the stuffing, as if one is wrapping a gift with traditional Korean wrapping cloth called *bojagi*. While the wraps might be a bit time-consuming to assemble, the results are delicious and the presentation is dramatic. The *ssam*'s delicate flavors and toothsome stuffing make this a special-occasion kimchi—perhaps for your Thanksgiving meal.

› Prep: 1 hour › Brine: 4 hours › Fermentation: 2 days › Makes 4 to 6 bossam kimchi

4 cups Mushroom Broth (page 26), soaked mushrooms reserved

Brine
1 large head (3 to 3 1/2 pounds) napa cabbage, halved lengthwise
8 cups water
1/2 cup kosher salt

Seasoning Paste
1 Asian pear, peeled, cored, and coarsely chopped
2 tablespoons minced garlic
2 tablespoons peeled, finely grated fresh ginger
2 tablespoons salted shrimp
2 tablespoons brine from salted shrimp
2 tablespoons anchovy sauce

6 ounces daikon radish (1/3 medium radish), julienned into 2-inch strips
2 medium Fuyu persimmons, peeled and quartered

6 raw peeled chestnuts (or water chestnuts), thinly sliced
2 tablespoons pine nuts
3 ounces Korean chives or 1/2 bunch European chives, cut into 2-inch pieces (about 1/4 cup)
20 flat-leaf parsley stems, cut into 2-inch pieces (about 1/3 cup)
10 Korean dates, pitted and thinly sliced, or 1/4 cup golden raisins
2 teaspoons chile pepper threads (see page 17), for garnish (optional)

Prepare the mushroom broth in advance and allow it to come to room temperature.

Spread apart the cabbage leaves, remove the inner yellow leaves, and set the halves aside. In a large bowl, or two large bowls, depending on the cabbage size, mix the water with the salt. Brine the cabbage halves at room

CONTINUED

temperature for 4 hours, using a heavy plate as a weight to keep the cabbage fully submerged. Rinse the cabbage halves in a bowl of cold water, cut off the bottoms, separate the leaves, and dry them thoroughly. Cut the reserved inner leaves into 1 1/2- to 2-inch flat squares (*nabak*-style, see page 22).

Thinly slice the reserved soaked mushrooms from the mushroom broth and set aside.

To make the seasoning paste, in a mini food processor fitted with a metal blade, combine the Asian pear, garlic, ginger, shrimp, shrimp brine, and anchovy sauce. Pulse until completely smooth and uniform.

In a large bowl, combine the seasoning paste with the radish, persimmons, chestnuts, pine nuts, chives, parsley, dates, and chile pepper threads. Add the inner cabbage leaves, and the reserved mushrooms, and mix well to combine.

Have ready a 2-quart container with a lid, or two 1-quart resealable bags. In a small soup bowl, arrange 4 to 5 outer leaves so that they resemble petals of a flower and overlap in the center. Trim and remove the bottom tough parts of the leaves (from the thick core) if they are not pliable. Place 1/2 cup of the stuffing mixture in the center of the cabbage leaves. Fold the overhanging cabbage leaves over the top, as if making a roll. Carefully transfer to the prepared container, then repeat with the remaining cabbage leaves and stuffing. Ladle the mushroom broth into the containers so that it covers the bottom one-third of the cabbage wraps. Cover, or if using bags, squeeze out the air and seal, and set aside for 1 day at room temperature. Refrigerate for at least 2 days and consume within 1 month.

To serve, partially unwrap the top leaf or cut into it to expose the stuffing.

Wrapped Seafood Kimchi

Bossam Kimchi (TRADITIONAL)

This kimchi contains seafood, which gives the *ssam* a briny flavor. While it's absolutely delicious, it's definitely for the daring and those who like bold seafood notes. This particular *ssam* doesn't need extended fermentation and storage and should be consumed within a couple weeks. It's a delicate alternative to a vegetable-based *ssam*, made to showcase the flavors of the sea. The stuffing is often made with a mixture of prized nuts, such as pine nuts or chestnuts, and fruits that celebrate fall's harvest.

› Prep: 1 hour › Brine: 8 hours or overnight › Fermentation: 1 day › Makes 4 to 6 bossam kimchi

Brine
1 large head (about 3 to 3 1/2 pounds) napa
    cabbage, halved lengthwise
8 cups water
1/2 cup plus 2 teaspoons kosher salt

4 cups Mushroom Broth (page 26), soaked
    mushrooms reserved

Seasoning Paste
1 Asian pear, peeled, cored, and coarsely chopped
2 tablespoons minced garlic
2 tablespoons plus 1 teaspoon peeled, finely
    grated fresh ginger
2 tablespoons salted shrimp
2 tablespoons brine from salted shrimp
2 tablespoons anchovy sauce

5 ounces baby octopus, cleaned and chopped into
    1/4-inch-thick strips, or rock shrimp or oysters
1/3 medium daikon radish, julienned into 2-inch
    strips (about 1/2 cup)
6 raw peeled chestnuts (or water chestnuts),
    thinly sliced

3 ounces Korean chives or 1/2 bunch European
    chives, cut into 2-inch pieces (about 1/4 cup)
20 flat-leaf parsley stems, cut into 2-inch pieces
10 Korean dates (see page 90), pitted and thinly
    sliced
2 tablespoons Korean chile pepper flakes
2 teaspoons chile pepper threads (optional)

Spread apart the cabbage leaves, remove the inner yellow leaves, and set the halves aside. In a large bowl, or two large bowls, depending on the cabbage size, mix the water with the 1/2 cup salt. Brine the cabbage halves at room temperature for 8 hours or overnight, using a heavy plate as a weight to keep the cabbage fully submerged. Rinse the cabbage halves in a bowl of cold water, cut off the bottoms, and let them drain in a colander for 15 minutes. Cut the reserved inner leaves into 1 1/2- to 2-inch flat squares (*nabak*-style, see page 22). In a medium bowl, toss the inner leaves with the remaining 2 teaspoons salt and let them brine for 15 minutes. Using a colander, rinse them under cold water to remove the salt and let drain for 15 minutes.

While the cabbage is brining, prepare the mushroom broth and allow it to come to room temperature. Finely chop the reserved soaked mushrooms and set aside.

Meanwhile, make the seasoning paste. In a food processor fitted with a metal blade, combine the Asian pear, garlic, ginger, shrimp, shrimp brine, and anchovy sauce. Pulse until completely smooth and uniform. Combine the seasoning paste with the octopus, radish, chestnuts, chives, parsley, dates, chile pepper flakes, and threads. Add the inner cabbage leaves and the reserved mushrooms and mix well.

Have ready a 2-quart container with a lid, or two 1-quart resealable bags. In a small soup bowl, arrange 4 to 5 outer leaves so that they resemble petals of a flower and overlap in the center. Trim and remove the bottom tough parts of the leaves (from the thick core) if they are not pliable. Place $^1/_2$ cup of the stuffing mixture in the center of the cabbage leaves. Fold the overhanging cabbage leaves over the top, as if making a roll. Carefully transfer to the prepared container, then repeat with the remaining cabbage leaves and stuffing. Ladle the mushroom broth into the containers so that it covers the bottom one-third of the cabbage wraps. Cover, or if using bags, squeeze out the air and seal, and set aside for 1 day at room temperature. Refrigerate for at least 2 days and consume within 2 weeks. To serve, partially unwrap the top leaf or cut into it to expose the stuffing.

Square-Cut Napa Cabbage Kimchi

Mak Kimchi (TRADITIONAL)

My mother tells me that, in Korea, early fall marked the arrival of the small, early-season cabbages that were harvested before they grew into larger, full mature heads of cabbage. With them, you made fresh kimchi and didn't have to wait a long time for it to be ready to eat. It was a kimchi meant to be eaten at every meal in anticipation of the napa cabbage season ahead.

In Korean, the word *mak* refers to the simple, everyday, casual, or common. And *mak* kimchi is just that—a simple, basic way to make kimchi and enjoy it freshly fermented. Instead of working with cabbage halves, which take weeks to ferment, as in *poggi* kimchi, you cut the cabbage into bite-size square pieces (*nabak*), and, after a quick dry-salt brine, toss it with the seasoning paste. The small pieces increase the surface area that's exposed to the seasoning, which, in turn, accelerates the fermentation process. *Mak* kimchi has become the most popular kimchi at restaurants and markets.

I recommend sampling this kimchi over time as it ages to get a full sense of the flavor spectrum within a single recipe. You can check the fermentation by opening the lid; you should see some bubbling juices and taste the tanginess of the freshly pickled cabbage. It will keep fermenting slowly in the jar for up to 6 months. The flavor will evolve and change with time—and a steady cold temperature and keeping the kimchi tightly packed in the jar will ensure an even, slow fermentation.

› Prep: 30 minutes › Brine: 1 hour › Fermentation: 3 days › Makes 8 cups (10 to 12 servings)

Brine
2 medium heads (about 4 to 6 pounds total) napa cabbage, cut into nabak shape (see page 22)
1/4 cup kosher salt

Seasoning Paste
1/2 cup thinly sliced yellow onion
4 teaspoons minced garlic
2 teaspoons peeled, finely grated fresh ginger
2 tablespoons anchovy sauce
2 tablespoons salted shrimp
2 teaspoons sugar
1/2 cup Korean chile pepper flakes

4 green onions, green parts only, cut into 2-inch pieces
1/4 cup water

In a large bowl, combine the cabbage with the salt and set aside for about 1 hour. Drain the liquid and rinse the cabbage to remove any traces of salt. Let the cabbage drain in a colander for 20 minutes, or use a salad spinner to remove most of the water.

Meanwhile, make the seasoning paste. In a mini food processor fitted with a metal blade, pulse together the onion, garlic, ginger, anchovy sauce, shrimp, and sugar until a paste forms. Transfer to a bowl and mix in the chile pepper flakes. Set aside for 15 minutes to let the flavors combine.

In a large bowl, mix together the green onions, seasoning paste, and drained cabbage until combined thoroughly, making sure the seasoning paste is distributed evenly among the leaves. Pack the mixture tightly into a 2-quart container. Add $^{1}/_{4}$ cup water to the mixing bowl, and swirl the water around to collect the remaining seasoning paste. Add the water to the container, cover tightly, and set aside for 3 days at room temperature. The cabbage will expand as it ferments, so be sure to place the jar on a plate or in a bowl to catch the overflow. Refrigerate and consume within 6 months.

MAKE IT VEGAN

To make a vegan version of *mak* kimchi, omit the anchovy sauce and salted shrimp, and instead add 3 tablespoons Mushroom Broth (page 26). If you do not want to use sugar or mushroom broth, puree $^{1}/_{2}$ peeled apple and add 2 teaspoons sea salt. Taste and adjust the seasonings before tossing the seasoning paste with the cabbage.

Savoy Cabbage Kimchi with Turnip

Yang Baechu Mak Kimchi (CONTEMPORARY)

In Korean, *mak* refers to a common, versatile style of kimchi making, where cabbage is cut into rough pieces, which allows it to ferment relatively quickly. Using Savoy cabbage gives this kimchi a range of texture and flavor very different from the Square-Cut Napa Cabbage Kimchi (page 78). Keep in mind that Savoy cabbage takes longer to ferment than green cabbage or napa cabbage because it has less water content. Green cabbage tends to be sweeter, too. (Properly brined cabbage should have a sweet taste with some salinity at the end; it's a pleasant taste, and shouldn't be too salty.) I've also started making this kimchi with turnips in lieu of daikon radish; I've found that turnips—which get softer faster than daikon radishes do—complement the cabbage in a similar way to how daikon radish goes with napa cabbage. Try using it in Chicken with Savoy Cabbage Kimchi, Lemon, and Olives (page 131) or the Friulian bean soup (page 140).

› Prep: 1¹/₂ hours › Brine: 1 hour 15 minutes, plus additional time depending on cabbage
› Fermentation: 5 days to 2 weeks in refrigerator › Makes 10 cups (8 to 10 servings)

Brine
1 large head (about 2 to 2¹/₂ pounds) Savoy cabbage, or green cabbage, cut into nabak shape (see page 22)

¹/₄ cup plus 2 teaspoons kosher salt

1 large (about 12 ounces) turnip, trimmed and cleaned, skin on

Seasoning Paste
²/₃ cup Korean chile pepper flakes

¹/₂ cup chopped yellow onion

¹/₄ cup anchovy sauce

2 tablespoons minced garlic

1 tablespoon peeled, finely grated fresh ginger

2 tablespoon salted shrimp

2 teaspoons sugar

³/₄ cup water

5 to 6 green onions, green part only, chopped into 1¹/₂-inch pieces (about 1 cup)

In a large bowl, toss the cabbage with the ¹/₄ cup salt. Set aside for 1 hour and 15 minutes. Check on the cabbage and if it looks wilted, limp, and slightly brighter in color, it is ready. Otherwise, give it another 15 minutes and check again. Rinse the cabbage and let it drain, shaking the colander a bit to remove excess moisture.

Meanwhile, cut the turnip into 1¹/₂-inch squares (*nabak*-style, see page 22). Try to duplicate the size of the cabbage pieces. In a medium bowl, toss the turnips with 1 teaspoon of the salt and set aside for 30 minutes. Rinse and pat the turnip pieces dry.

While the cabbage continues to brine, prepare the seasoning paste. In a mini food processor fitted with a metal blade, pulse together the chile pepper flakes, onion, anchovy sauce, garlic, ginger, shrimp, and sugar until the mixture is uniform and resembles hummus. Add $^1/_4$ cup of the water and pulse until incorporated. Taste and adjust the seasonings.

In a large bowl, toss together the cabbage, turnips, and green onions. Add the seasoning paste and toss together until the paste coats all the vegetables evenly.

Pack the vegetables tightly into about 5 pint- or quart-size jars. Add $^1/_2$ cup water with the remaining 1 teaspoon salt to the seasoning bowl and swirl the water around to collect the remaining seasoning paste. Distribute the water among the jars, cover, and allow to sit at room temperature for 5 days. Refrigerate and allow the flavors to develop for about 2 weeks. Eat within 6 months. The cabbage will keep fermenting slowly for up to 6 months, and its taste will evolve and change with time.

MAKE IT VEGAN

For a vegan version of this recipe, substitute the following mixture for the seasoning paste. Follow the recipe instructions to prepare the seasoning paste.

Vegan Seasoning Paste
$^2/_3$ cup chopped yellow onion
$^3/_4$ cup Mushroom Broth (page 26)
$^1/_2$ cup Korean chile pepper flakes
2 tablespoons minced garlic
1 tablespoon peeled, finely grated fresh ginger
1 tablespoon sugar, plus more to taste

Mother-in-Law's Signature Kimchi

Baechu Gutjori (TRADITIONAL)

Traditionally Koreans celebrate the first of the fall napa cabbage harvest with this kimchi. Called *gutjori,* this "instant" kimchi is seasoned liberally and eaten fresh (before fermentation and aging) just prior to *kimjang*, the annual fall harvest. Despite *gutjori's* customary "instant" readiness, I've found that it's more delicious when allowed to ferment longer than typically called for. To me, the longer strips of cabbage (compared to Square-Cut Napa Cabbage Kimchi on page 78) make them better suited for longer fermentation. The viscous, rich seasoning with beef stock, this kimchi's signature ingredient, complements the fresh cabbage and the seasoning paste, which results in a depth, length, and roundness. Just as in many French recipes, it's the stock that provides the backbone to the rich, layered flavors. Mother-in-Law's original house recipe hails from my mother's restaurant, Jang Mo Jip (see page 3), and transcends a particular regional style of kimchi making. I like to describe our *gutjori* kimchi as "Basque," because it marries the flavors of land (beef stock) and the flavors of the sea (oysters, salted shrimp, and anchovy sauce), which creates wonderful, complex flavors. See for yourself—eat it while it's fresh, and then again after it ages in the fridge for a few weeks or months to determine which you prefer.

› Prep: 30 minutes › Brine: 1 hour 35 minutes › Fermentation: Ready to eat or 2 to 3 days and up to 1 year, depending on your preference › Makes 8 cups (10 to 12 servings)

Brine
2 medium heads (4 to 5 pounds total) napa cabbage
2 tablespoons kosher salt

Seasoning Paste
2 tablespoons salted shrimp
1/3 cup Sweet Rice-Flour Porridge (page 24)
1/4 cup anchovy sauce
1/4 cup Beef Stock (page 25)
2 tablespoons minced garlic
1 tablespoon peeled, finely grated fresh ginger
2 teaspoons sugar
2/3 cup Korean chile pepper flakes

1/2 cup thinly sliced yellow onion
4 green onions, green parts only, cut into 2-inch pieces (about 1/2 cup)
3 ounces Korean chives or 1/2 bunch European chives, cut into 4-inch pieces (about 1/4 cup)
6 to 8 fresh oysters (optional)

Cut the cabbage into quarters, and then cut each quarter in half lengthwise and cut out the core. Lay each cabbage segment flat, then quarter into sections about 1 inch wide by 6 inches long. If some of the leaves are too wide, cut them to approximate proportions. In a large bowl, toss the cabbage with the salt and set aside to brine for 1 hour and 15 minutes. Rinse off the salt in a bowl of cold water and let the cabbage leaves drain in a colander for 20 minutes.

To make the seasoning paste, in a mini food processor fitted with a metal blade, puree the shrimp, porridge, anchovy sauce, stock, garlic, ginger, and sugar. Transfer the mixture to a bowl and add $1/4$ cup of the chile pepper flakes and mix by hand. Let the seasoning paste sit for 15 minutes to let the flavors combine.

In a large bowl, toss the cabbage, onion, green onions, and chives with the remaining chile pepper flakes until the chile pepper flakes lightly coat the vegetables. Add the seasoning paste and oysters and mix until evenly distributed. Pack tightly into a 2-quart container, cover, and set aside for up to 2 days at room temperature. Then move the container to a refrigerator. You can also eat the kimchi immediately, but I prefer the slightly aged, fermented taste. As it ferments, cabbage will expand, so be sure to place the jar on a plate or in a bowl to catch the overflow.

Daikon Radish Cube Kimchi

Kkakdugi (TRADITIONAL)

Daikon radish (*muu* in Korean) is widely used in kimchi and other Korean dishes. A hearty root vegetable that thrives in the cool months, daikon radish has a long tradition of being turned into kimchi called *kkakdugi*. The bite-size cubes showcase the spicy, thick sauce that marries so well with radish's crunchy, juicy, refreshing texture.

After napa cabbage kimchi, *kkakdugi* is one of the most beloved and commonly consumed types of kimchi, and it can be purchased in grocery stores year-round. Covered in a thick seasoning paste, *kkakdugi* is boldly spicy and crunchy, at first. It retains its heat after a long wintertime fermentation, even after it sours into a tangy, almost pineapple-like pickle. Because of its density, the daikon gives off more carbon dioxide as it ferments, resulting in a pungent odor. But don't let its strong scent deter you. Because it releases a lot of juice during fermentation, the daikon requires a bit more sugar.

Kkakdugi is also famous for being the best kimchi accompaniment to a beloved Korean soup called *seollungtang,* made with beef brisket and bone marrow. *Seollungtang* is especially served as a breakfast soup, and is a specialty at my mother's restaurant. My mother tells me that a *seollungtang* restaurant's reputation may be based solely on how good their *kkakdugi* tastes. Try this crunchy kimchi as an accompaniment to the Mother-in-Law's Porchetta sandwich (page 121). Or you can also add *kkakdugi* to chili or roasts, as you would a turnip (like in Braised Short Ribs with Bachelor Radish Kimchi, page 135), to uplift flavors in your favorite winter dishes.

> ›Prep: 30 minutes ›Brine: 30 minutes ›Fermentation: 3 to 4 days ›Makes 8 cups (10 to 12 servings)

Brine
4 pounds daikon radishes (about 2 to 3 large)
2 tablespoons kosher salt

Seasoning Paste
1/2 cup Sweet Rice-Flour Porridge (page 24)
2 tablespoons salted shrimp
1 tablespoon minced garlic
2 teaspoons peeled, finely grated fresh ginger
1 tablespoon sugar
2/3 cup Korean chile pepper flakes
1/4 cup Beef Stock (page 25; optional)

4 green onions, green parts only, cut into 1-inch pieces (about 1/2 cup)
1/3 cup water

Using a paring knife, trim the radishes and scrape away the outer grimy layer. Do not peel the entire outer layer of the radish; the skin is needed to maintain firmness while pickling. Cut the radishes into 3/4- to 1-inch cubes—it's okay if some pieces aren't exact.

CONTINUED

In a large colander, sprinkle the radish cubes with the salt and let them brine for 30 minutes. Drain the radishes and set them in the colander over a bowl to drain some more.

Meanwhile, make the seasoning paste. In a mini food processor fitted with a metal blade, pulse together the porridge, shrimp, garlic, ginger, and sugar until a paste forms. Transfer the mixture to a medium bowl and stir in the chile pepper flakes and stock. Set aside for about 15 minutes to let the flavors combine.

In a large bowl, combine the drained radishes with the seasoning paste and green onions until the seasoning paste is evenly distributed throughout. Pack tightly into two quart-size containers. Add about $1/3$ cup water to the mixing bowl and swirl the water around to collect the remaining seasoning paste. Add a few tablespoons of the water to each container. Cover tightly and let sit at room temperature for 3 to 4 days. Refrigerate and consume within 6 months.

Bachelor Radish Kimchi

Chonggak Kimchi (TRADITIONAL)

Chonggak literally translates as "bachelor radish" but is also known as "ponytail radish" because its long greens resemble ponytails. The term *chonggak kimchi* stems from the name of the young radish, *chonggak muu,* which has greens resembling the ponytails of young Korean boys (*chonggak*) in days past. *Chonggak* kimchi is a classic winter kimchi that is traditionally fermented in *onggi* pots in Korea along with White Stuffed Cabbage Kimchi (page 89) and Daikon Radish Halves Pickled in Clear Broth (page 95). Because the dense root vegetable is kept whole, this kimchi holds up well to long-term aging. Growing up, this was one of my favorite kimchi to eat.

As winter gets underway, the flavor and texture of these radishes grows deeper, and all the while the radishes retain a nice crunch and tanginess. *Chonggak* are eaten in their entirety along with their greens, which also stay crunchy. At the New Amsterdam Market in New York City, we turned many of our customers on to this kimchi, so much so that many customers would say, "I'll take the bachelor." It became an instant favorite.

› Prep: 1¹/₂ hours › Brine: 1 hour › Fermentation: 3 to 4 days › Makes 8 cups (10 to 12 servings)

Brine
4 pounds bachelor radishes with their greens
   (see tip, page 88)
¹/₂ cup kosher salt

Seasoning Paste
³/₄ cup Sweet Rice-Flour Porridge (page 24)
¹/₄ cup anchovy sauce
¹/₄ cup salted shrimp
3 tablespoons minced garlic
2 tablespoons peeled, finely grated fresh ginger
1 tablespoon sugar
³/₄ cup Korean chile pepper flakes

Using a vegetable peeler or a paring knife, trim the root part of the radishes. Rinse the radishes in several changes of cold water and drain (radishes tend to be very gritty, so take care to thoroughly clean them). Sprinkle the radishes and greens with the salt and brine for 1 hour. Rinse well under running cold water. Or rinse in a large bowl filled with water until all of the salt is removed.

Meanwhile, to make the seasoning paste, in a mini food processor fitted with a metal blade, pulse together the porridge, anchovy sauce, shrimp, garlic, ginger, and sugar. Transfer the mixture to a bowl and stir in the chile

CONTINUED

pepper flakes. Set aside the seasoning paste for 15 minutes to let the flavors combine.

In a large bowl, combine the radishes with the seasoning paste and mix until the paste is evenly distributed. Pack the radishes tightly into a half-gallon container, layering them on top of one another if necessary, and wrapping the greens around the root end. Cover tightly and let sit at room temperature for 3 to 4 days. Refrigerate and consume within 6 months.

TIP

You can find bachelor radishes in the fall in Korean markets. If they're not easy to find, substitute French Breakfast or table radishes—they're a good alternative, although the flavor of the radishes themselves will be milder (so you'll need to adjust the amount of seasoning paste accordingly). Due to their more delicate root and stem, they will not hold up to long-term fermentation, so consume within 1 week, if substituting radishes.

White Stuffed Cabbage Kimchi

Baek Poggi Kimchi (TRADITIONAL)

Baek means "white" in Korean, and that is exactly how this kimchi looks—it doesn't have the usual red color. This no-spice, no-chile-pepper-flake kimchi is an homage to what most kimchi in Korea was like up until the introduction of chile peppers in the seventeenth century. Before you discount the no-spice, plain white kimchi, consider the appeal of a pure, crisp taste of cabbage, delicately complemented by the earthy notes of pine nuts and dates. Its fresh taste and tangy, fermented broth (delicious pickle juice) is a delicious contrast to the spicy, bold chile pepper flavors of winter kimchi and hearty stews. This kimchi recipe requires square, flat containers or wide-mouth gallon or half-gallon pickle jars—you will be stuffing them with cabbage halves.

› Prep: 1 hour › Brine: 8¹/₂ to 11¹/₂ hours › Fermentation: 4 days
› Makes 4 cabbage halves (about 16 servings)

Brine
2 large heads napa cabbage (about 6 to 7 pounds total), yellow leaves discarded, halved lengthwise
1 cup plus 1 teaspoon kosher salt

Seasoning Paste
1 medium yellow onion, chopped
¹/₄ cup minced garlic
2 tablespoons peeled, finely grated fresh ginger
¹/₄ cup Mushroom Broth (page 26)

1¹/₂ pounds daikon radish (about 1 medium), julienned into 3-inch strips
1 Asian or Bosc pear, peeled, cored, and julienned
1 cup thinly sliced carrot (about 2 carrots)
4 dried shiitake mushrooms, rehydrated in Mushroom Broth (page 26) and thinly sliced
¹/₂ cup pine nuts (optional)

¹/₂ cup thinly sliced dried Korean dates (about 12 dates), or golden raisins
2 tablespoons chile threads (optional)
2 tablespoons black sesame seeds (optional)
¹/₂ cup water

Generously sprinkle ¹/₄ cup of the salt over the cabbage halves, making sure the salt is on top of the core, the outer base, the thickest part, and between the individual leaves. Stack the cabbage halves in a large bowl or a wide and deep stockpot, layering the halves on top of one another. Let the cabbage dry brine for 30 minutes. Fill the bowl or stockpot with just enough cold water to cover the cabbage, add ³/₄ cup of the salt, and stir to dissolve. Taste the water—it should taste like the sea. Brine the cabbage at room temperature for 8 to 10 hours or overnight with a heavy plate on top to ensure

CONTINUED

that the cabbage stays submerged, turning the cabbage over midway through for even brining. As it brines, the cabbage will wilt, shrink, and sink. If, after 10 hours, the outside bottom leaves are still firm, let the cabbage brine for an additional hour and check again. Brine until the leaves look wilted.

Once brined, lift the cabbage out of the water and drain. Fill another large bowl with water and rinse out the salted cabbage, gently agitating while submerged. Shake it out well and drain in a colander in the sink or over a dish rack with the cut side facing down, for at least 40 minutes. The leaves should taste slightly salty-sweet, and the colors should look brighter than they did before brining.

Meanwhile, prepare the seasoning paste. In a mini food processor fitted with a metal blade, puree together the onion, garlic, and ginger. Add the broth and pulse until a paste forms. Transfer the contents to a large bowl and combine with the radishes, pear, carrot, mushrooms, pine nuts, dates, chile threads, and sesame seeds.

Take one of the cabbage halves and spread a generous amount of the stuffing between the leaves, working from the outermost leaf inward and making sure the stuffing is applied between each layer of leaves. Slather the stuffing on the cut side of the cabbage then fold the leaves over the cut side. Repeat this process for each half.

Carefully pack the cabbage halves as tightly as possible into the containers, making sure to keep the stuffing intact. Add $1/2$ cup water to the mixing bowl and swirl the water around to collect the remaining seasoning paste. Add the remaining 1 teaspoon salt to the water, and distribute the water equally among the containers. If there is a gap between the cabbage and the lid, and add additional water to cover. Make sure the cabbage is submerged. Seal tightly. Let sit at room temperature, away from direct light, for 4 days. Refrigerate and consume within 6 months.

NOTE

Korean dates, called *daechu* (pictured opposite), are dried jujube fruit that grows throughout Asia and India, Nepal, and the Middle East. They naturally turn red when dried, and impart a nutty, fruity flavor that works well in kimchi recipes—particularly in white kimchi.

Stuffed Cabbage Kimchi

Poggi Kimchi (TRADITIONAL)

This is the most traditional version of cabbage kimchi made during *kimjang* (the fall cabbage harvest), and it's intended to last through the winter months. *Poggi* kimchi refers to stuffed cabbage halves, which are brined overnight and then slathered with a well-seasoned stuffing paste. Keeping the cabbage halves intact ensures that fermentation occurs at a steady, slow pace—perfect for optimizing the flavors of the cabbage. *Poggi* kimchi varies in its style and taste depending on the region—southern regions use more seafood, and northern ones use less. This is the most basic version of the recipe, highlighting the pure flavors of slowly fermented kimchi. If you plan to make a smaller batch than the recipe yields, use at least one head of cabbage. The more you make, the better the fermentation will be. If you only use half a cabbage, the low volume will affect the fermentation and diminish the overall result.

These days we mostly use wide-mouthed gallon-size glass jars, which allow the kimchi to ferment at room temperature for the initial stage of fermentation, before moving it to the refrigerator. It's important for your jars to have a wide opening as you have to be able to fit half a head of cabbage through the opening. You can also use a lidded 1-gallon plastic tub or pickle jar.

The beauty of *poggi* kimchi is that the cabbage half is kept intact until just prior to serving, which is when you cut it into bite-size pieces. Cutting *poggi* kimchi before serving is akin to carving a steak at the table—the practice is somewhat of a ritual in Korean culture. By cutting *poggi* kimchi just before serving, you honor your guests by serving them the freshest pieces of cabbage brimming with tangy fermentation. The moment you cut into the cabbage half, you release the optimal flavor and aroma. In a Korean household, you would never serve leftover, precut *poggi* kimchi to your guests. Instead, it would go into a soup or a stew.

› Prep: 1 hour › Brine: $8^1/_2$ to $11^1/_2$ hours, or overnight › Fermentation: 4 to 5 days
› Makes 4 cabbage halves; 1 gallon (about 16 servings)

Brine
2 large heads napa cabbage (about 6 to 7 pounds total), yellow leaves discarded, halved lengthwise
1 cup kosher salt, divided

Seasoning Paste
$1/_4$ cup salted shrimp
$1/_4$ cup anchovy sauce
$1/_4$ cup Sweet Rice-Flour Porridge (page 24)

3 tablespoons minced garlic
1 tablespoon peeled, finely grated fresh ginger
2 teaspoons sugar
1 cup Korean chile pepper flakes
$1^1/_2$ pounds daikon radish, (about 1 medium) julienned into 3-inch strips
$1/_2$ cup water

CONTINUED

Generously sprinkle $1/4$ cup of the salt over the cabbage halves, making sure the salt is on top of the core, the outer base, the thickest parts, and between the individual leaves. Stack the cabbage halves in a large bowl or a wide and deep stockpot, layering the halves on top of one another. Let the cabbage dry brine for 30 minutes. Fill the bowl or stockpot with just enough cold water to cover the cabbage, add the remaining salt, and stir to dissolve. Taste the water—it should taste like the sea. Brine the cabbage at room temperature for 8 to 10 hours or overnight with a heavy plate on top to ensure that the cabbage stays submerged, turning the cabbage over midway through for even brining. As it brines, the cabbage will wilt, shrink, and sink. If, after the 10 hour brine, the outside bottom leaves are still firm, let the cabbage brine for an additional hour and check again. Brine until the leaves look bright green but wilted.

Once brined, lift the cabbage out of the water and drain. Fill another large bowl with water and rinse out the salted cabbage, gently agitating while submerged. Shake it out well and drain in a colander in the sink or over a dish rack with the cut side facing down, for at least 40 minutes. The leaves should taste slightly salty-sweet, and the colors should look brighter than they did before brining.

Meanwhile, prepare the seasoning paste. In a mini food processor fitted with a metal blade, pulse together the shrimp, anchovy sauce, porridge, garlic, ginger, and sugar until smooth. Transfer the mixture to a large bowl and mix in the chile pepper flakes and radish. Let sit for 15 minutes.

Take one of the cabbage halves and spread a generous amount of the stuffing between the leaves, working from the outermost leaf inward, and making sure the stuffing is applied between each layer of leaves and the innermost core. Slather the stuffing on the cut side of the cabbage then fold the leaves over the cut side. Repeat this process for each half.

Carefully pack the cabbage halves as tightly as possible into the containers, making sure to keep the stuffing intact. Add the water to the mixing bowl and swirl it around to collect the remaining seasoning paste; distribute the water equally among the containers. If there is a gap between the cabbage and the lid, add additional water to cover. Make sure the cabbage is fully submerged. Cover tightly. Let sit at room temperature, away from direct light, for 4 to 5 days. Refrigerate and consume within 1 year.

Daikon Radish Halves Pickled in Clear Broth

Dongchimi Kimchi (TRADITIONAL)

This recipe is another winter favorite, also traditionally made during *kimjang*. One of my most vivid childhood memories is being sent out in the cold to my grandmother's backyard to retrieve kimchi from the *onggi* jar. I remember gently tapping and breaking the thin layer of ice that had formed on top, the crackling sound that followed, and the chill of *dongchimi* kimchi juices underneath. I can still taste, in my memory, the crisp, bracing acidity of the radish juice.

This refreshing white kimchi is a perfect contrast to hot, spicy soups and hearty wintry meals. Koreans prize the deep, savory, clean flavors of the radish and carefully choose the best, youngest, and most tender radishes for this kimchi. The juices are precious and are saved for use later as a summer soup base in dishes such as *nengmyung* (buckwheat noodle) soup. Here I'm sharing with you my *emo*'s ("aunt" in Korean) secret recipe that calls for boiled potato water to ensure a crisp daikon radish. Now it'll be *our* secret.

› Prep: 20 minutes › Brine: 16 hours › Fermentation: 1 week at room temperature and 3 weeks in the refrigerator › Makes 1 gallon (10 to 12 servings)

3 pounds daikon radishes (about 3 small or 2 medium), greens attached and farm-fresh if possible
1/2 cup kosher salt
3 large cloves garlic, halved
1-inch piece ginger, peeled, halved, and cut into 1/8-inch-thick slices
1/2 medium yellow onion, peeled and quartered
1/2 Asian pear, peeled, cored, and quartered
1 jalapeño pepper, halved, seeded, and cut into 1/2-inch slices
3 green onions, white and light green parts only, cut into 2-inch pieces (about 1/2 cup)
6 cups water
1 medium russet potato, peeled

Rinse the radishes. Using a vegetable brush, clean the dirt off the radish skins, but do not peel the outer layer, which provides an important layer of protection during the long fermentation period. Halve the radishes lengthwise, keeping the greens intact.

In a large mixing bowl, sprinkle 1/4 cup of the salt over the radish halves, and let stand at room temperature for 16 hours. Drain.

Tightly pack the radishes in a gallon-size container. Place the garlic, ginger, onion, pear, jalapeño, and green onions on top.

In a 4-quart pot, combine the water, potato, and the remaining 1/4 cup salt. Bring to a rolling boil, and then cook the potato for 10 minutes. Discard the potato, and pour the hot water over the radishes in the container. Cover tightly. Let sit at room temperature, away from direct sunlight, for 1 week. Refrigerate and let ferment for at least 3 weeks before consuming.

Just prior to serving, slice the radishes in half again lengthwise (so they are in quarters), then cut into 1/2-inch pieces. Divide among bowls and ladle the juices over the radishes.

COOKING WITH KIMCHI

Korean cooking, like many traditional cuisines, makes use of every ingredient in the pantry—nothing goes to waste. Wilted vegetables are tucked into soups and stews, and tough cuts of meat are braised for a long time. This resourcefulness is particularly true with aged kimchi, which has always been treated as a precious ingredient and a flavoring agent, something that couldn't be carelessly discarded.

As a raw, naturally fermented food, kimchi continues to age indefinitely, its flavors intensifying from a simple melody into a complex symphony over time. The well-aged, fermented flavors of older kimchi are considered valuable in cooking. Households have reserved one-year-old, even two-year-old *poggi* kimchi made during the *kimjang* harvest for use in cooking special stews.

Decades ago, before Koreans had household refrigerators (and certainly before modern kimchi refrigerators), it wasn't uncommon for two-year-old kimchi to be retrieved from the *onggi*, rinsed, and chopped up for a soup, stew, *ssam*, or pancake. Just as you would scrape off an unsavory spot from a wedge of cheese that might have lingered in your fridge, old kimchi was never thrown out. A precious, valued ingredient, it was always treated with respect.

The deep, developed flavors you get with older kimchi add tremendous flavor notes to a wide range of dishes. The more intensely flavored the kimchi, the deeper the flavors that appear in the dish. These potent, fermented, tangy flavors of kimchi can never be replicated with another ingredient—they are complex, layered flavor notes that boldly or subtly enhance your dish. While you can add acidity using lemon, lime juice, or vinegar, the natural acidity that comes from kimchi's fermentation is all its own.

Of course, when you talk about cooking with kimchi, the first dish that comes to mind is one of Korea's most treasured:

Kimchi Chigae Stew (page 138). When I'm really tired, jet–lagged, or have just returned from an exhausting trip, the dish that I immediately make, the dish that brings me back and revives me, is a well-braised kimchi *chigae*. For me, it's the security blanket of comfort foods—it has no other match—and it's my equivalent of a nourishing and restorative chicken soup. Since there's always some aged, fermented kimchi in the back of my fridge, I make this for myself whenever I need an extra bit of comfort in my bowl.

Because of its acidity, kimchi is an excellent complement to rich-tasting foods such as flank steak, pork belly, or pork shoulder; or briny, pungent seafood like mussels and flaky fish. It offers delicious flavor and complexity. It can take the spotlight, as it does in a preparation with steak and chimichurri (page 132), or play a backup role enhancing the main ingredients, as it does in Kimchi Risotto (page 112). Even when you cook kimchi, its natural acidity and brightness shine through. That effervescence, that brightness, has always reminded me of what I taste when I have a glass of crisp white wine, such as Riesling.

By using kimchi in lieu of lemongrass to enhance the flavors in Red Curry Mussels with Kimchi (page 127), the dish acquires deeper sour notes, contrasting nicely with the rich sweetness of coconut milk. And by adding kimchi to chicken with lemon and olives (page 131), you'll get a dish layered with notes that complement the briny Mediterranean olives.

When cooking with kimchi, don't overlook the kimchi juice, which is a versatile and indispensable ingredient that can enrich so many dishes. By kimchi juice, I mean the liquid that forms in the jar while kimchi ferments. From Kimchi Oyster Mignonette (page 128) or a Kimchi Grapefruit Margarita (page 141), to a marinade and glaze for Kimchi Oven-Baked Baby Back Ribs (page 137), kimchi juice is an invaluable ingredient because

› Most recipes in this chapter called for aged kimchi; be careful when measuring the kimchi that you don't include the juice (unless it's called for), as the extra liquid will throw off the recipe. For recipes that do call for kimchi juice, feel free to use any kind of Fall/Winter kimchi juice that you have on hand.

of its acidity and flavor. I collect my kimchi juice and use it for cooking in numerous ways (it will keep for a year or so). When reduced with sugar, the juice cooks down to a rich, tangy, savory-sweet syrup that turns into a delicious glaze for baby back ribs, but there's no reason why you can't use it on burgers or kebabs.

While some of the recipes here use kimchi from the Spring/Summer chapter for a lighter touch, many of the recipes use napa cabbage and daikon radish kimchi from the Fall/Winter chapter because they have fermented for longer and thus have deeper, more layered flavors. What I want to demonstrate here is just how versatile kimchi is as an ingredient: in salads, soups, stews, sandwiches, and beyond.

While a lot of the recipes call for napa cabbage kimchi because it's the most common, feel free to experiment with other types of kimchi. Napa cabbage's versatility comes from its soft, juicy texture that blends easily with flavors in other dishes. Daikon radish kimchi has a texture that works well in braises, stews, and soups. Each type of cabbage—napa, Savoy, green—has its own distinct flavor and texture, especially as it ages, and will bring a different quality to a recipe. When you cook with these different kimchi, you'll be able to discern the flavors and textures of the vegetables.

Generally the kimchi called on as an ingredient in this chapter should be a well-fermented, aged kimchi—one that's aged for at least one month in your refrigerator, but two to three months is best, as it will yield a deep fermented umami flavor that adds layers of flavors to the dish. Fresher kimchi will produce a different, milder result with more texture, but, most likely, less flavor. You will also discover how even a six-month-old or older "vintage" kimchi can suddenly come to life when you cook with it; its lifeless cabbage leaves become viscous when sautéed with olive oil, allowing its sweet, smoky, and mellowed umami flavor to shine through.

> Because some of the recipes require kimchi juice, and because aged kimchi is used in cooking, you might want to consider making double batches of kimchi from the Fall/Winter chapter once you become comfortable with making kimchi.

With this chapter, I hope you will begin to view kimchi as a valuable ingredient and not just as a delicious side dish or condiment. This chapter only scratches the surface of kimchi's breadth and scope, and I am confident you can build on it and begin to experiment using kimchi as an ingredient in your own recipes.

Kimchi Frittata with Green Onions and Shiitakes

Kimchi and eggs is one of those meant-to-be combinations. The creamy richness of eggs contrasts nicely with the sharp tang of kimchi combined with mushrooms and green onions. The flavors and texture play perfectly off one another.

I enhanced photographer Jessica Boucher's kimchi frittata recipe from the MILKimchi website. To make the frittata silky-smooth and fluffy, cooking it at a low oven temperature. Remove your frittata from the oven while the center is still a bit loose—it will finish cooking as it cools. Kimchi gives this classic combination a tartness that, combined with the delicate, soft egg custard, makes the frittata rich and decadent. Serve this frittata warm with a piece of country bread—and more kimchi on the side, of course.

› Prep: 30 minutes › Serves 4 as an appetizer

3 tablespoons extra-virgin olive oil

6 shiitake mushroom caps, thinly sliced, or 1/2 cup fresh cremini mushrooms, cleaned and thinly sliced

2 green onions, green and white parts, sliced thinly and diagonally (about 1/4 cup)

1/4 teaspoon kosher salt, plus more to taste

1/3 cup Green Onion Kimchi (page 55) or any napa cabbage kimchi, cut into 1-inch pieces

4 large eggs

1/4 cup whole milk

1 teaspoon Korean chile pepper flakes (optional)

Position the rack in the middle of the oven and preheat to 250°F.

Heat 2 tablespoons of the oil in an 8-inch ovenproof skillet over medium-high heat until the oil is shimmering. Add the mushrooms and green onions and cook with a pinch of salt for 5 minutes, until the mushrooms are soft. Add the kimchi and cook for another 2 minutes, until the kimchi is warmed through. Remove from heat and set aside for 2 minutes.

In a medium bowl, whisk together the eggs, milk, and remaining salt. Pour the egg mixture over the mushrooms and kimchi in the skillet, sprinkle the chile pepper flakes over the egg mixture, and place the skillet in the oven.

Bake for 15 to 17 minutes, until the eggs are just set, but still quiver slightly in the center. Remove the skillet from the oven and serve immediately for a soft frittata or allow to cool and serve at room temperature.

Eggs Benedict with Kimchi Hollandaise

I heard about the famed kimchi hollandaise at the restaurant Michael's Genuine, in Miami, from my yoga teacher, Elena Brower. Being a fan of poached eggs, I wanted to re-create it at home to see what it tasted like. The rich, eggy, buttery hollandaise sauce seemed like a perfect canvas for kimchi's brightness. Adding kimchi juice gave it a subtle spice and acidity, which is a nice contrast to the lusciousness of poached eggs. You can also serve the hollandaise with steamed or roasted asparagus.

› Prep: 15 to 20 minutes › Serves 4

4 pieces Canadian bacon or ham

Kimchi Hollandaise
3 large egg yolks, lightly beaten
Squeeze of fresh lemon juice
1 1/2 tablespoons kimchi juice
1/4 teaspoon kosher salt
1/4 teaspoon Korean chile pepper flakes
1/2 cup (1 stick) unsalted butter, melted until foamy

4 large eggs
2 English muffins, split open for toasting
Unsalted butter
1 cup any napa cabbage kimchi, chopped, for garnish
Finely chopped European chives, for garnish

Warm a large skillet over medium-low heat. Add the Canadian bacon and cook, turning occasionally, 5 to 7 minutes, until lightly browned on both sides. Transfer to a plate lined with paper towels and set aside.

To make the hollandaise, in a blender, combine all of the hollandaise ingredients except for the butter and mix well. With the blender on high speed, add the butter in a slow, steady drizzle, until the mixture is smooth and thoroughly combined. Transfer the hollandaise to a serving dish and set aside.

Fill a medium bowl with ice water and set aside. In a large wide saucepan, bring 4 inches of water to a boil. Reduce the heat to medium-low until the water is just simmering. Working with 1 egg at a time, break the egg into a small heatproof bowl. Gently tip the bowl toward the simmering water and slide the egg into the water. Using a large spoon, cover the yolk with some of the egg white. Repeat with the remaining eggs. When the eggs grow opaque after about 4 minutes, using a slotted spoon, gently remove them from the water and place in the ice water. Transfer to a cutting board and trim the frayed edges to create a smooth shape.

As soon as the eggs are done cooking, toast the English muffins. Butter one half of each toasted English muffin and top it with a piece of Canadian bacon. Place a poached egg on top of the Canadian bacon and spoon some hollandaise sauce on top. Garnish with a piece of kimchi and chives and serve.

Corn Salad with French Breakfast Radish Kimchi

The combination of fresh sweet corn and the piquant, crunchy French Breakfast radish is the highlight of summer. French Breakfast Radish Kimchi (page 51), with its verdant radish tops, is the perfect side dish to grilled meat and picnic dishes. Tangy kimchi juice highlights corn's inherent sweetness in this simple, truly spectacular summer salad. Serve some with grilled fresh peaches for a sweet and savory combination that will remind you of summer all year long.

› Prep: 30 minutes › Makes 4 cups (4 servings)

6 ears corn, shucked

8 radishes from French Breakfast Radish Kimchi (page 51)

20 flat-leaf parsley leaves

1/4 cup slivered red onion

1/4 cup kimchi juice from the French Breakfast Radish Kimchi (page 51)

2 tablespoons extra-virgin olive oil

Kosher salt

Fill a large bowl with ice water and set aside. Bring a large pot of salted water to a boil over high heat. Add the corn and cook for 3 minutes. Remove the corn and place in the ice water to cool. Transfer to a colander to drain for 5 minutes. Cut off the kernels and discard the cobs.

In a large bowl, combine the corn kernels, radishes, parsley, and onion. In a small bowl, stir together the kimchi juice and olive oil. Let stand for 3 minutes. Toss the dressing with the vegetables until combined. Add salt to taste. Serve immediately at room temperature or refrigerate for 2 to 4 hours before serving.

Kimchi Cornmeal Pancakes

A popular Korean side dish, these delicious, savory pancakes are usually made with green onion and mung beans, a yellow lentil-like legume, and served as an appetizer. I was inspired to make a more accessible pancake, using cornmeal, because I think a savory pancake with kimchi should be simple. Use either green onion or chive kimchi, or any aged cabbage kimchi you have on hand. The smoky, tangy flavors of this pancake are addictive.

› Prep: 30 minutes › Makes 2 (10-inch) pancakes (serves 4 as an appetizer)

Dipping Sauce
2 tablespoons soy sauce
1 tablespoon unseasoned rice vinegar
1 tablespoon toasted sesame oil

Pancakes
2/3 cup all-purpose flour
1/3 cup coarse cornmeal
2 tablespoons sweet rice flour
1 1/2 cups cold seltzer water or ice-cold water
2 cups Green Onion Kimchi (page 55) or any aged cabbage kimchi, liquid drained and coarsely chopped
2 tablespoons vegetable or other neutral oil

To make the dipping sauce, stir together the soy sauce, rice vinegar, and sesame oil in a small bowl.

To make the pancakes, in a medium bowl, stir together the all-purpose flour, cornmeal, and sweet rice flour. Add the seltzer water and stir until just incorporated. Add the kimchi and mix to combine. The batter texture should be similar to a smoothie.

In a 10-inch nonstick pan, heat 1 tablespoon of the oil over medium-high heat until it shimmers. Make sure the surface is hot and well covered with oil. Using a ladle, pour half of the batter into the center of the skillet and slowly smooth the batter toward the outer edges of the skillet. Cook for 2 to 3 minutes, until the edges are crispy, and then carefully flip the pancake with a spatula and cook for another 1 to 2 minutes, until nicely browned. To make your pancakes crispier, press down gently with your spatula until you hear a sizzle. Remove the pancake from the pan and allow to cool for 2 minutes, then cut into wedges. Repeat with the remaining batter and the remaining 1 tablespoon oil.

Serve the hot pancake wedges with the dipping sauce alongside.

Cold Sesame Noodle Salad with Kimchi

Cold noodles on a hot summer day are a perfect no-fuss, almost-no-cooking-needed treat. It is my go-to meal in the summer and one of my all-time favorite comfort foods. While in the winter I have Kimchi Chigae Stew (page 138) to revive and comfort me, in the summer I make these refreshing cold noodles. Perhaps it's because this dish transports me right back into my childhood that I find it so satisfying to combine the chopped kimchi, with its piquant, tangy spice, and cold noodles slathered with nutty toasted sesame oil. If you like a little background sweetness, add a little sugar. If you prefer to add salad to these noodles, toss in some table radishes or julienned cucumbers and mesclun greens.

› Prep: 15 minutes › Makes 2 servings (serves 4 as a side dish)

3 tablespoons toasted sesame oil

2 teaspoons soy sauce

1/4 cup kimchi juice

1 teaspoon sugar (optional)

2 bundles (7 ounces total) soba or rice noodles

1 cup any cabbage kimchi, Quick Cucumber and Chive Kimchi (page 41), or Deconstructed "Stuffed" Eggplant Kimchi (page 57), chopped

8 sprigs European chives, chopped into 2-inch pieces, for garnish (optional)

In a large bowl, combine the sesame oil, soy sauce, kimchi juice, and sugar. Stir well and set aside.

Cook the noodles according to the package instructions, drain, and rinse under cold running water to cool completely. Let drain for a few minutes more. Combine the noodles with the kimchi and the soy sauce mixture. Toss together to mix well and serve immediately, garnished with the chives.

Pan-Fried Kimchi Dumplings (Mandu)

Compared to other Asian dumplings, Korean *mandu* (dumplings) have a generous amount of tofu curds along with meat and vegetables, which makes for a lighter dumpling. In Korea, every family has a different *mandu* recipe, especially families from the North, where dumplings probably migrated from China, and there's even a saying, "If your family is from the North, they make the best dumplings." *Mandu* are served steamed or fried, and also appear in a popular rice cake dumpling soup that is customarily served on New Year's Day. In this recipe, we serve the dumplings pan-fried and tapas-style, intended to be one of many small bites.

› Prep: 3 hours › Makes 8 to 10 servings as an appetizer (55 to 60 dumplings)

Dumplings
1 (14-ounce) package firm tofu
3¹/₂ teaspoons kosher salt
¹/₂ head (about 1 pound) green cabbage, cored and quartered
¹/₂ pound mung bean sprouts (omit if unavailable)
2 cups any napa cabbage kimchi, finely chopped
¹/₂ pound ground beef, preferably sirloin
2 large eggs
2 tablespoons toasted sesame oil
Freshly ground black pepper
Dumpling or gyoza wrappers
1 large egg white
Neutral cooking oil, for frying
Water, for steaming

Dipping Sauce
1 tablespoon unseasoned rice vinegar
2 tablespoons soy sauce

Place the tofu in cheesecloth and squeeze the tofu into a ball to remove as much moisture as possible. Transfer the tofu to a large bowl and set aside. Set aside the cheesecloth.

In a large pot over high heat, bring 3 inches of water and 1 teaspoon of the salt to a boil. Add the cabbage and boil for 6 minutes, until limp. Drain the cabbage in a colander set over a sink, and rinse under cold running water to cool completely. Chop the cabbage finely and, using cheesecloth, squeeze out as much moisture as you can. You want the tofu and all the filling components to be as dry as possible. Transfer the chopped cabbage to the bowl with the tofu.

Bring another batch of water to a boil and add the bean sprouts and 1 teaspoon of the salt. Cook for about 3 minutes, until the sprouts are soft. Remove the pot from the heat and drain in a colander set over a sink; rinse the sprouts under cold running water to cool completely. Chop the sprouts finely and, using cheesecloth, squeeze out as much moisture as you can. Transfer the chopped sprouts to the bowl with the tofu and cabbage.

Add the kimchi, beef, eggs, sesame oil, pepper, and the remaining salt to the bowl with the tofu and cabbage. Mix until thoroughly combined.

CONTINUED

Place $1/2$ tablespoon of the mixture in the center of a dumpling wrapper. Using your fingers, moisten the edges of the wrapper with the egg white, and fold the wrapper over, making a semicircle. Press down gently on the edges to seal them. Repeat until no filling remains.

Over medium-high heat, warm 2 tablespoons of the cooking oil in a large cast-iron skillet until the oil is shimmering. Add 10 to 12 dumplings to the skillet and cook, making sure they are well coated in oil, until they are nicely browned, 2 to 3 minutes per side. Lower the heat to medium and add $1/4$ cup water to the skillet. Cover and steam the dumplings for 4 to 5 minutes, until they are plump and lightly browned with a crust on the outside. Monitor the skillet carefully to make sure that you do not burn off all the water, as it is easy to burn the dumplings at this stage. Repeat the process until all the of dumplings are cooked.

Meanwhile, make the dipping sauce. In a small bowl, stir together the rice vinegar and soy sauce. When the dumplings are ready, serve them hot, along with the dipping sauce.

FREEZING DUMPLINGS

If you don't want to cook all of the dumplings at once, you can freeze the remaining filling. Alternatively, you can make all the dumplings with the filling and wrappers, and freeze the extra dumplings by placing them on a baking tray (make sure they don't touch and freeze together) and flash freezing them for 20 minutes. After that, you can place them loosely into a container or a plastic bag to store in the freezer.

Fry frozen dumplings for 4 to 6 minutes per side. Be careful when frying frozen dumplings, as the oil might sputter and sizzle. It's critical to make sure that each dumpling is well coated in oil as the oil will create a "seal" for the steaming phase when you cover the skillet. When you get to the steaming stage, add $1/3$ cup water and steam for 7 to 9 minutes to get the desired results.

Kimchi Slaw with Cilantro

This crowd-pleasing kimchi slaw is perfect either for those who enjoy kimchi but can't handle the heat or a first-time kimchi eater. It marries bold kimchi flavors with cilantro, lime, and mild kimchi spice. The slaw is versatile as a side salad for a barbecue or with fried chicken, and it makes a great hot dog topping. Add some shredded chicken and it becomes a main course. If you need more crunch, throw in some fresh sweet corn and thinly sliced radishes. For a more dramatic flavor, swap in perilla (see page 53) or shiso leaves instead of cilantro. Use the neutral oil if you want the dressing to coat the slaw.

› Prep: 10 minutes › Makes 4 servings

4 cups shredded green cabbage or red cabbage
   (or both)
1¹/2 cup Daikon Radish Cube kimchi (page 85)
   and/or any napa cabbage kimchi, chopped
4 green onions, thinly sliced diagonally
¹/4 cup chopped cilantro, or thinly sliced perilla
   or shiso leaves
Juice of ¹/2 lime
¹/4 cup kimchi juice
1 tablespoon neutral oil (optional)

In a large bowl, combine the cabbage, kimchi, green onions, and cilantro.

In a small bowl, whisk together the lime and kimchi juices. Slowly whisk in the oil until well incorporated.

Pour the dressing over the cabbage mixture and toss to coat. Serve immediately, or cover and refrigerate for a few hours to let the flavors meld further.

Kimchi Risotto

After conquering the perfect pasta, mastering risotto opened up new possibilities for me to understand how to flavor rice. This dish focuses on the simplicity of combining Parmesan cheese and kimchi, creating a fine balancing act of flavors. With its orange color, creamy Arborio rice, and sharp Parmesan, kimchi risotto is a delicious way to showcase kimchi's depth of flavor in a classic Italian dish.

› Prep: 40 minutes › Makes 6 servings

1 quart chicken or vegetable stock, plus more if needed
3 tablespoons extra-virgin olive oil
6 tablespoons unsalted butter
1 large yellow onion, finely diced
2/3 cup any cabbage kimchi, finely chopped
1 pound Arborio rice
1 cup dry white wine
1/2 teaspoon kosher salt
1/4 teaspoon freshly ground black pepper
1 cup (4 ounces) freshly grated Parmigiano-Reggiano
Finely chopped European chives, for serving

Put the stock in a 2-quart pot with a lid and place over medium heat.

In a large stockpot over low heat, warm the olive oil and 2 tablespoons of the butter. Add the onion and cook for 6 minutes, without letting the onion brown. Add the kimchi and cook, stirring, for 3 minutes more. Add the rice and increase the heat to medium-high. Stir the rice until it begins to look translucent, about 1 minute. Add the wine, season with salt and pepper, and continue stirring until the rice has absorbed the wine.

Once the wine has been absorbed, turn the heat to low, and add the salt and 1 ladle of stock and cook, stirring, until it has been absorbed by the rice. Add another ladle of stock, cooking and stirring until it has been absorbed. Continue the process for 15 to 20 minutes. Taste the rice periodically; by the time it is done, it should be soft, but have a slight bite (al dente). If 1 quart of stock isn't enough, have more warm stock on hand to complete the job; it could take another ladle or so. (If you've run out of stock, you can add some boiling water to the mixture.)

Remove the risotto from the heat; stir in the remaining butter and the Parmigiano-Reggiano until well incorporated. Divide among bowls, garnish with chives, and serve immediately.

Farro and Butternut Squash Kimchi with Lacinato Kale and Ricotta Salata

This is a delicious, healthy, wholesome fall grain salad featuring Butternut Squash Kimchi with Lacinato Kale and Pine Nuts (page 69), which complements the nuttiness of farro (a type of cereal grain) perfectly. It is a beautiful salad, with greens, vibrant orange color, and barley flavors that are spectacular and unexpectedly lively. If you want to highlight tender springtime flavors, use French Breakfast Radish Kimchi (page 51) instead. The possibilities of this dish are endless—add vegetables such as yellow squash, green or yellow beans, or brussels sprouts and some grated ricotta salata cheese and you have a balanced, flavorful main course salad.

› Prep: 1 hour (including soaking time) › Makes 4 servings

1 cup farro
1²/₃ cups water
¹/₄ teaspoon kosher salt
1 cup coarsely chopped Butternut Squash Kimchi
  with Lacinato Kale and Pine Nuts (page 69),
  or French Breakfast Radish Kimchi (page 51),
  preferably aged at least 3 days
¹/₂ large red bell pepper, seeded and thinly sliced
  into 2 inch slivers (about ¹/₂ cup)
1 tablespoon extra-virgin olive oil
3 tablespoons freshly grated ricotta salata, feta,
  or goat cheese
Kosher salt
Freshly ground black pepper

In a medium bowl, cover the farro with water and soak for 20 minutes. Drain the farro in a colander. In a medium pot, bring the water and the salt to a boil. Add the farro, decrease the heat to low, and simmer, uncovered, for 25 minutes, until the grains are puffed. Using a colander, drain the water and let the farro cool to room temperature.

In a large bowl, toss together the farro, kimchi, bell pepper, and oil. Season with salt and pepper to taste. Serve immediately or refrigerate until ready to serve.

Kimchi Fried Rice Dolsot-Style

When my cousin, Cathy, makes this recipe, she fries the rice so that it forms a delicious, crispy crust. Her version is a riff on a traditional dish called *dolsot bibimbap*, in which rice is cooked in a stone bowl and forms a crispy bottom layer. By sautéing the kimchi to the point where it develops a slightly caramelized crust, the kimchi develops a nice smoky flavor. Be sure to use a well-aged kimchi, one that is at least two months old, and use dry day-old cooked rice, which works better than fresh, steamed rice. By folding in lightly whisked eggs and some peas, this simple fried rice becomes beautiful, sumptuous, and satisfying.

› Prep: 20 minutes › Makes 4 servings

2 large eggs
Pinch of kosher salt
1 tablespoon neutral cooking oil
1/2 cup finely chopped yellow onion
2 tablespoons toasted sesame oil
2 tablespoons unsalted butter
3 cups day-old rice, at room temperature
1 1/2 cups aged napa cabbage kimchi with its juice
    (at least 2 months old), coarsely chopped
1/4 cup kimchi juice
1/2 cup frozen petite peas
Freshly ground black pepper (optional)

In a medium bowl, gently whisk the eggs with a pinch of salt. In a small, nonstick skillet set over medium heat, warm the cooking oil, then cook the eggs, gently stirring with a spatula, for 3 minutes, being careful not to overcook. Remove from the heat and set aside.

In a large skillet over medium heat, cook the onion with the sesame oil until translucent, 3 to 5 minutes. Transfer to a bowl and set aside.

Return the skillet to the stove and increase the heat to medium-high. Melt the butter and stir in the rice. Cook for 3 minutes. Add the kimchi and kimchi juice and cook, stirring, until both the rice and kimchi are cooked through and well combined, 4 to 5 minutes.

Let the rice and kimchi cook, undisturbed, so that they form a nice crust on the pan. Once a crust forms, begin to stir and press down on the mixture so that you get lots of fried bits, repeating continuously for 6 to 8 minutes. The rice mixture should be fluffy.

Add the frozen peas and cook for 2 minutes. Stir in the eggs and onion, and remove from the heat immediately. Serve right away, with a pinch of freshly ground black pepper.

Roasted Brussels Sprouts with Cipollini Onion Kimchi

Chef David Chang of Momofuku made brussels sprouts with bacon and kimchi puree famous. To highlight the vegetables even more, I eliminated the bacon and added apples, pine nuts, and Cipollini Onion Kimchi (page 56) for additional sweet and tangy notes. They worked beautifully, and I didn't miss the bacon. If you prefer to use napa cabbage kimchi instead, puree it and toss it with the roasted brussels sprouts just before serving, as Chef Chang would do.

› Prep: 1 hour › Makes 2 to 4 servings

1 pound brussels sprouts, trimmed and halved lengthwise

1 medium firm apple (such as Gala or Fuji), peeled, cored, and diced

1 cup Cipollini Onion Kimchi (page 56), with a few tablespoons of kimchi juice

3 tablespoons extra-virgin olive oil

Kosher salt

3 tablespoons pine nuts

Position a rack in the middle of the oven and preheat to 400°F.

In a large bowl, toss the brussels sprouts, apple, and kimchi with the oil. Season to taste with salt.

Spread the brussels sprouts mixture on a rimmed baking sheet and roast for 45 minutes. Halfway through roasting, add the pine nuts and stir to ensure even browning. Serve warm.

Scalloped Potatoes with Kimchi

Instead of roasting the potatoes in the oven, here they are cooked in a gratin sauce on the stove top and finished under the broiler. The combination of potatoes, cheese, and heavy cream with tangy, spicy kimchi works brilliantly. You may use Chive Kimchi (page 54), Green Onion Kimchi (page 55), or any cabbage kimchi, but be sure not to layer the kimchi on top because it might burn. Top with grated cheese, finish under the broiler, and voilà!—in less than 30 minutes you have creamy, decadent potatoes with just the right bite.

› Prep: 45 minutes   › Makes 6 servings

Unsalted butter, for greasing the pan

3 pounds thin-skinned potatoes (such as Yukon gold), sliced 1/16 inch thick

1 teaspoon kosher salt

Freshly ground black pepper

3/4 cup Chive Kimchi (page 54), Green Onion Kimchi (page 55), or any cabbage Kimchi, coarsely chopped

1 cup heavy cream

1/2 cup coarsely grated Parmigiano-Reggiano

Preheat the broiler. Generously butter a 10-inch cast-iron pan with a lid. Place a layer of potatoes in the pan in an overlapping pattern (layer any thicker pieces on the bottom of the pan to cook more evenly) and season with the salt and pepper to taste. Add 1/4 cup of the kimchi, followed by 1/3 cup of the cream and 2 tablespoons of the cheese. Repeat this process 2 times, ending with cheese as the final layer.

Cover the pan tightly, and cook on the stove top over medium heat for 20 minutes. Sprinkle the remaining cheese over the potato layers then broil until the cheese browns, about 8 to 10 minutes. Serve immediately.

Winter Greens with Kimchi

As much as I love soups, stews, and other comfort foods in the winter, I still miss eating greens during those cold months. Kale is a staple vegetable, and when combined with garlic and kimchi, it's even more delicious. This is a nice diversion from standard winter sautéed vegetables, and it adds a kick to your hearty greens.

› Prep: 10 minutes › Makes 4 side-dish servings

1 bunch (12 ounces) Lacinato kale, or another kale
   or Swiss chard
2 tablespoons extra-virgin olive oil
4 cloves garlic, slivered
1/2 cup any cabbage kimchi or Daikon Radish Cube
   Kimchi (page 85), finely chopped with juice
Squeeze of lemon juice (optional)
Freshly grated Parmigiano-Reggiano (optional)

Trim the bottom 2 inches off the kale and slice the leaves into 3/4-inch ribbons. In a large skillet over medium-high heat, warm the oil. Add the garlic and cook until golden brown, about 3 minutes. Add the kimchi and kale and cook, stirring, until the kale is wilted, 3 to 5 minutes.

Transfer the mixture to a large bowl. Drizzle lemon juice over the greens and sprinkle with the Parmigiano-Reggiano before serving.

Turkey "Banh Mi" with Kimchi

Traditional *banh mi* uses pork, but I wanted to try something a little off the traditional Vietnamese path. I swapped ground turkey for pork and used a summery kimchi in place of vinegared vegetables and spicy mayonnaise. Cooking the meat with kimchi seasonings amplifies the flavor combination of garlic, ginger, and spice that is the backbone of Southeast Asian flavors and complements the gamey taste of turkey. Quick Cucumber and Chive Kimchi (page 41) works well in this dish if you're looking for an alternative to napa cabbage. If you can't find ground turkey, ground chicken (dark meat) or ground pork also work well. Your days of take-out *banh mi* might just be numbered.

▸ Prep: 20 minutes   ▸ Makes 4 to 6 servings

1/2 cup mayonnaise
1/4 cup chopped cilantro
2 tablespoons neutral cooking oil
1 tablespoon finely chopped garlic
1 teaspoon peeled, finely grated fresh ginger
1 pound ground turkey
2 tablespoons anchovy sauce or fish sauce
1 teaspoon Korean chile pepper flakes
1 teaspoon sugar
1 cup Tender Young Napa Cabbage Kimchi
    (page 47), Korean Radish Top Kimchi
    (page 48), or any napa cabbage kimchi, finely
    chopped, plus more for garnish
2 green onions, green and white parts, chopped
    (about 1/4 cup)
Juice of 1/2 lime (about 1 tablespoon)
2 tablespoons kimchi juice
2 baguettes cut into thirds, or 4 (8-inch) rolls,
    split open
Cilantro sprigs
1 cup thinly sliced cucumbers (optional)
1 cup shredded carrots (optional)

In a small bowl, stir together the mayonnaise and the cilantro. Set aside.

In a large skillet over medium-high heat, warm the oil. Add the garlic and ginger and cook, stirring, for 1 minute. Add the turkey and cook, breaking up the meat with a wooden spoon, until the meat is no longer pink, about 5 minutes. Stir in the anchovy sauce, chile pepper flakes, and sugar. Remove from the heat and stir in the kimchi, green onions, lime juice, and kimchi juice. Let the mixture stand for 3 minutes, then stir in half of the cilantro mayonnaise.

Spread the remaining mayonnaise mixture on the split bread. Spread the turkey mixture on the bread and add sprigs of cilantro, the cucumbers, carrots, and kimchi for garnish. Serve immediately.

The Mother-in-Law's Porchetta

Chef Sara Jenkins has been a fan of MILKimchi since our launch, and serves our kimchi alongside her renowned porchetta at her New York restaurant. When I walk by Porchetta, I've often noticed that customers add our kimchi in their sandwiches.

Here, I've adapted the complementary Mediterranean flavors of fennel and sage to kimchi by introducing a dipping sauce made with chile pepper flakes and salted shrimp—a classic pairing with pork in Korean tradition. Pork, a staple in both Italian and Korean cooking, is a perfect canvas for kimchi in an Italian-style sandwich topped with daikon radish kimchi. You can also try it as a *bossam*-style lettuce wrap, which is traditionally served with pureed napa cabbage kimchi, steamed rice, and lettuce leaves for wrapping (page 132).

› Prep: 5 hours › Makes 8 to 12 servings

Rub
1 tablespoon fennel seeds
1 tablespoon Korean chile pepper flakes
1 tablespoon salted shrimp
4 large cloves garlic, minced
1/2 cup extra-virgin olive oil

1 (5 1/2- to 6-pound) pork shoulder with bone
1 tablespoon kosher salt
1 tablespoon freshly ground black pepper
2 tablespoons sherry vinegar
1 cup water

Dipping Sauce
1 tablespoon extra-virgin olive oil
1 tablespoon brine from salted shrimp
2 teaspoons sherry vinegar
1 teaspoon peeled, finely grated fresh ginger
1 teaspoon Korean chile pepper flakes
1 green onion, green parts only, chopped
   (about 1 tablespoon)

2 cups Daikon Radish Cube Kimchi (page 85),
   chopped, or any napa cabbage kimchi, chopped
   or pureed

Preheat the oven to 450°F. To make the rub, in a small mixing bowl, stir together the fennel seeds, chile flakes, salted shrimp, garlic, and olive oil until well combined. Set aside half of the mixture for the dipping sauce.

Using a sharp knife, make about ten 1/2-inch-deep slits all over the pork. Season the pork with the salt and pepper. Using half of the rub for the meat, stuff about half into the slits then rub the remainder all over the meat evenly.

Put the pork in a large Dutch oven or casserole dish. Place in the oven and cook uncovered for 45 minutes. Remove from the oven and lower the oven temperature to 250°F. Add the 2 tablespoons sherry vinegar and the water to the Dutch oven and return to the oven. Cook the shoulder for 4 hours, until tender, basting the pork every hour with its juices. Trim the fat and discard. Use a fork to shred the meat.

Meanwhile, make the dipping sauce. In a small bowl, mix the reserved rub mixture with the olive oil, brine, vinegar, ginger, chile pepper flakes, and green onion.

Serve the kimchi alongside the pork, accompanied by the dipping sauce.

Grilled MILKimcheeze Sandwich

Anne Saxelby and I became friends after she shared her story about making kimchi while in junior high for a science project. Being fascinated with kimchi and fermentation ever since, Anne opened Saxelby Cheesemongers in New York City. We soon collaborated on a kimchi and cheese tasting, pairing three versions of napa cabbage kimchi ranging in age from one to nine months, with a mild cow cheese and a blue cheese to complement the different levels of fermentation and strength of flavors. We also took daikon kimchi and paired it with fresh goat cheese; it was fascinating to try two completely different fermented products side by side and taste the difference in flavor brought out in the kimchi by fresh goat cheese versus aged cow cheese.

And from that experiment, a recipe for grilled cheese with kimchi—MILKimcheeze—as we called it, was first prepared on a warm spring day at a charity event for the New Amsterdam Market, our local monthly outdoor market. It has quickly become an all-time favorite! Also try this with kimchi that is sautéed before it's added to the grilled cheese sandwich for a mellower flavor.

› Prep: 5 minutes › Makes 4 servings

1/4 cup unsalted butter
8 (1/2-inch-thick) slices country-style bread
16 ounces cheese, such as Havarti, Monterey jack, or Swiss, sliced thick
1 cup any napa cabbage kimchi, coarsely chopped

Heat the griddle or a large skillet over medium-low heat.

Butter the slices of bread on one side and place them on the skillet, butter side down (you may need to do this in batches). Distribute the cheese evenly on half of the bread slices and cook until slightly melted. Place the kimchi on top of the cheese, top with the remaining toasty bread slices, and cook for 1 minute more, or until the cheese is completely melted and the bread is toasted golden brown. Using a spatula, gently flip the sandwich and cook for 1 minute longer. Remove from the pan and cut each sandwich in half for easier handling. If working in batches, repeat with the remaining ingredients. Serve hot.

The Mother-in-Law Kimchi Brisket Sandwich

After I asked for a sandwich suitable for our kimchi, Matt Ross and Eric Finkelstein of Court Street Grocers in Brooklyn gave me their take on the ultimate brisket sandwich adapted from recipes from their respective mothers using Korean kimchi, Jewish brisket, and Italian broccoli rabe and garlic bread. Affectionately called "The Mother-in-Law," this is no ordinary sandwich. Perfect as a main course for a football party on a wintry day, it's a no-holds-barred sandwich: rich brisket, bitter rabe, and fragrant garlic bread combined with the brightness of kimchi will make our mothers and current and future Mother-in-laws proud.

› Prep: 3¹/₂ hours › Makes 8 sandwiches, with plenty of brisket left over

1 bunch (about 12 ounces) broccoli rabe, cut into
   3-inch-long pieces, or 4 cups broccoli florets,
   chopped
¹/₄ cup extra-virgin olive oil
2 large cloves garlic, sliced
1 teaspoon Korean chile pepper flakes
1 teaspoon anchovy sauce
Pinch kosher salt (optional)

Brisket
2 tablespoons neutral cooking oil
1 (3- to 4-pound) brisket (both flat and point cuts
   work well)
1 small yellow onion, thinly sliced
1 clove garlic, minced
1¹/₂ tablespoons peeled, finely grated fresh ginger
1 star anise (optional)
1 cup ketchup
¹/₂ cup soy sauce
¹/₃ cup sherry vinegar
¹/₂ cup sugar
1 cup water

Garlic Butter
4 cloves garlic
¹/₄ teaspoon kosher salt
¹/₂ cup (1 stick) unsalted butter, softened
Handful of fresh flat-leaf parsley

8 ciabatta rolls, or any soft, airy, moderately
   crusty roll
²/₃ cup mayonnaise
2 cups Mother-in-Law's Signature Kimchi
   (page 82), chopped

Position a rack in the middle of the oven and place a rimmed baking sheet on it. Preheat the oven to 450°F. In a medium bowl, toss the broccoli rabe with the olive oil, garlic, chile pepper flakes, anchovy sauce, and salt. Transfer the rabe to the hot baking sheet and roast, stirring midway, until the rabe starts to caramelize, 16 to 18 minutes. Remove from the oven and set aside.

To make the brisket, decrease the oven temperature to 325°F. In a 6-quart Dutch oven set over medium-high heat, add 1 tablespoon of the cooking oil and brown the brisket on all sides, 6 to 8 minutes per side. Remove the brisket and set aside. Drain and discard the rendered fat.

Decrease the heat to medium and add the remaining 1 tablespoon cooking oil and the onion to the Dutch oven and cook, stirring, until translucent and lightly browned, 5 minutes. Add the garlic, ginger, and star anise and cook for 30 seconds. Stir in the ketchup, soy sauce, sherry vinegar, and sugar and combine until a thick sauce forms. Add the water to the sauce and stir until bubbling. Place the brisket back in the Dutch oven with the fat side up, cover, and place in the oven. The braising liquid should reach about one-third of the way up the brisket. If the liquid level is low, add water. Braise for $2^{1}/_{2}$ to 3 hours, until very tender.

Meanwhile, make the garlic butter. In a food processor fitted with a metal blade, pulse the garlic and salt together until combined. Add the butter and parsley and pulse just until incorporated.

Transfer the brisket to a cutting board, cover with foil, and let rest for 20 minutes. Reserve the braising liquid. Slice the brisket thickly, against the grain.

To assemble the sandwiches, slice each roll in half and spread each half with the garlic butter. As soon as the brisket comes out of the oven, place the rolls in the oven on a baking sheet (you may have to do this in batches), cut sides up, and bake until the butter melts and the rolls are lightly toasted, about 10 minutes. Remove the rolls from the oven and spread a layer of mayonnaise on both cut sides of the rolls and drizzle with some of the reserved braising liquid. Evenly distribute the roasted broccoli rabe over 4 rolls, then the brisket slices, and then the kimchi. Top with the other half of the roll, press down lightly with your hands, and serve immediately.

TIP

If not serving right away, place the brisket slices in an ovenproof dish and spoon some of the sauce over them. Cover the dish with foil and refrigerate until ready to use. To reheat before serving, preheat the oven to 325°F and place the brisket in the oven for 5 to 8 minutes.

To assemble the sandwiches, with the oven still at 325°F, place the sliced brisket in a large ovenproof dish in a single layer, cover with the reserved braising liquid, and warm for 3 to 5 minutes, until the liquid begins to bubble.

Red Curry Mussels with Kimchi

A perfect complement to briny seafood, kimchi stands in for the tanginess of lemongrass and lime in this Thai-inspired curry. I love the result—brothy and creamy, with tart underlying kimchi notes. Be sure to serve it with crusty bread to soak up the delicious broth.

› Prep: 10 minutes   › Makes 4 servings

1/4 cup unsalted butter

1 tablespoon peeled, finely grated fresh ginger

2 large cloves garlic, minced

2 tablespoons Thai red curry paste

1 cup any napa cabbage kimchi, coarsely chopped, plus more for garnish

2 (14-ounce) cans coconut milk

1/2 cup white wine

4 pounds mussels, rinsed and scrubbed

1/4 cup kimchi juice

2 green onions, white and green parts, finely chopped (about 1/4 cup), for garnish

In a 5-quart Dutch oven or heavy-bottomed pot, melt the butter over medium-high heat. Add the ginger and garlic and cook for 30 seconds to 1 minute, until aromatic. Add the curry paste and kimchi and cook, stirring, for 1 minute. Stir in the coconut milk and wine and bring the mixture to a simmer.

Reduce the heat to low, add the mussels, and cover. Cook for 5 to 7 minutes, until the mussels open.

Remove the pot from the heat and stir in the kimchi juice. Top with the green onions and kimchi and serve in deep bowls.

TIP

Mussels are delicious, but there are a few safety guidelines you should keep in mind when preparing these bivalves. When cleaning the mussels, if you find any that are slightly open, gently tap on them. If the mussel closes, it's alive and safe to eat. If the mussel stays open, throw it away. Throw away cracked or damaged mussels, too. Any mussels that refuse to open after cooking should not be eaten.

Kimchi Oyster Mignonette

Kimchi juice is so versatile—it should never be discarded. In addition to being a terrific ingredient in margaritas (page 141), marinades, or a glaze for baby back ribs (page 137), kimchi juice is a great way to uplift oyster mignonette. Kimchi brine continues to ferment in a jar if you set it aside in the refrigerator; I keep mine for months. Its spicy, tangy flavorful liquid is a perfect complement to the natural salinity of an oyster. I'll take this recipe and some fresh oysters with a crisp glass of Muscadet anytime!

› Prep: 5 minutes › Makes a little over 3 tablespoons of mignonette, enough for at least 1 dozen oysters

1 tablespoon rice vinegar
$^1/_2$ teaspoon minced shallot
$^1/_2$ teaspoon peeled, finely grated fresh ginger
2 tablespoons kimchi juice
1 dozen fresh shucked oysters

In a small bowl, combine the rice vinegar, shallot, ginger, and kimchi juice. Stir well and serve alongside the oysters.

Flounder with Brown Butter, Capers, and Kimchi

One of my all-time favorites dishes at Balthazar, an institution in New York City, is its French brasserie variation of Sole Meunière. I've loved that dish for many years and almost always order it when I find myself there. One day I was trying to re-create the recipe at home and wondered what the dish would taste like with kimchi. I added sautéed kimchi, capers, and white wine to the brown-butter sauce, giving this classic a delicious kimchi twist. The sautéed kimchi and its juice add a lift and cut the richness of the butter. If you cannot find flounder, you may substitute trout or catfish.

› Prep: 20 minutes › Makes 2 servings

3 tablespoons unsalted butter
1/2 cup any napa cabbage kimchi, finely chopped
1 tablespoon chopped capers
1 tablespoon chopped shallot
1/4 cup white wine
2 flounder fillets (12 to 16 ounces total)
Kosher salt
Freshly ground black pepper
1/2 cup all-purpose flour
1 tablespoon neutral cooking oil
Lemon juice, for serving (optional)

In a small skillet over low-medium heat, melt 1 tablespoon of the butter until foamy. Add the kimchi, capers, and shallot and cook, stirring, for about 2 minutes, or until translucent. Add the white wine and 1 tablespoon of the butter and cook for 1 minute longer. Remove from the heat and set aside.

Rinse the fish and pat dry with paper towels, removing any excess moisture. Liberally season the fish with salt and pepper. In a medium bowl, dredge the fish fillets in the flour, shaking off the excess.

In a large skillet over medium-high heat, melt the remaining 1 tablespoon of the butter with the oil until the mixture gets foamy. Place the fillets in the skillet skin-side down and cook until the bottom of the fish is golden brown, about 3 minutes.

After the first side of the fish is done, using a wide, thin spatula, carefully flip the fillets over and continue to cook for another 2 to 3 minutes, until the other side is golden brown.

Plate the fish, spoon the butter sauce over the fish, and serve.

Spanish Mackerel with Green Onion Kimchi and Potatoes

Green Onion Kimchi (page 55) or Tender Young Napa Cabbage Kimchi (page 47), with their mild spring/summer kimchi flavors, work particularly well with flavorful Spanish mackerel. A versatile fish, Spanish mackerel takes well to hearty, spicy potatoes and red bell peppers, and it reminds me of a dish I ate in Spain or Portugal. Adding some spicy chorizo intensifies the flavors even further. You may also make this dish with rainbow trout or blue fish instead of mackerel.

› Prep: 20 minutes › Makes 4 servings

4 Spanish mackerel fillets (about 1 pound)
1 teaspoon plus a pinch kosher salt
Freshly ground black pepper
3 tablespoons neutral cooking oil
1 medium yellow onion, thinly sliced
1 large clove garlic, finely chopped
1 teaspoon peeled, finely chopped fresh ginger
3 small white potatoes (about 12 ounces),
    peeled and finely diced
1/2 cup white wine
1 cup Green Onion Kimchi (page 55) or Tender
    Young Napa Cabbage Kimchi (page 47), aged
    for at least 2 weeks, chopped into 3-inch pieces
1/4 cup kimchi juice
1/2 red bell pepper, seeded and thinly sliced into
    2-inch slivers (about 1/2 cup)
2 teaspoons soy sauce
2 teaspoons Korean chile pepper flakes
1 teaspoon sugar
2 or 3 green onions, green parts only, sliced into
    2-inch pieces (about 1/4 cup)
Flat-leaf parsley, chopped, for garnish (optional)

Pat dry the fish fillets to remove any excess moisture. Season the fish with a pinch of salt and pepper.

In a large sauté pan over medium-high heat, warm 2 tablespoons of the oil and cook the fish, skin side down, until lightly browned, 2 to 3 minutes per side. Remove the fish and set aside.

Add the remaining oil to the pan and add the onion, garlic, ginger, and 1 teaspoon of the salt. Cook, stirring, until the onion is translucent, about 2 minutes. Add the potatoes and cook, stirring, until the potatoes are slightly golden, about 5 minutes. Add the wine to the pan and simmer for 1 minute.

Add the kimchi, juice, bell pepper, soy sauce, chile pepper flakes, and sugar and stir for 3 minutes, until well incorporated with the vegetables. Reduce the heat to medium and add the mackerel and green onions, spooning the sauce over the fish for another 2 minutes.

Plate the fish with the vegetable mixture on the bottom and the fish on top. Garnish with the parsley. Serve warm.

Chicken with Savoy Cabbage Kimchi, Lemon, and Olives

I love pan-sautéed chicken thighs, which produce delicious cooking juices that make for a sumptuous sauce when simmered with white wine. A combination of Savoy cabbage kimchi, lemon peel, and olives gives this dish a Moroccan flare that will transport you to a Mediterranean climate, especially during the dead of winter. Napa cabbage kimchi can also work here, but the dish will be more tangy, so adjust accordingly by adding a bit of raw Savoy cabbage or kale to help offset the intensity of the tangy flavors.

› Prep: 30 minutes › Makes 4 servings

4 bone-in skin-on chicken thighs (about 1¹/₂ to
　2 pounds)
¹/₄ teaspoon plus a pinch kosher salt
Freshly ground black pepper
2 tablespoons extra-virgin olive oil
2 cloves garlic, sliced
1 medium yellow onion, thinly sliced
¹/₂ cup dry white wine
1 cup finely chopped Savoy Cabbage Kimchi with
　Turnip (page 80), without juice
¹/₂ cup green olives, pitted
4 (2-inch) strips lemon peel, pith removed and
　julienned

Position a rack in the middle of the oven and preheat the oven to 350°F. Wash and pat dry the chicken and season with a pinch of salt and pepper.

In a large ovenproof skillet set over medium-high heat, warm 1 tablespoon of the olive oil until it's shimmering. Add the chicken, skin-side down first, and cook until the fat has rendered and it is brown on both sides, about 4 minutes per side. Transfer to a plate and set aside.

Drain the fat from the skillet, being careful not to splatter. Add the remaining oil, ¹/₄ teaspoon salt, the garlic, and onion and cook for 2 to 3 minutes. Add the wine and simmer for 2 minutes, until reduced by half. Add the kimchi and olives and cook for 5 minutes more.

Transfer the chicken back to the skillet and coat with the garlic, onion, kimchi sauce, and lemon peels. Cover the skillet and finish cooking in the oven for 20 minutes, until the juices run clear when the thigh is pierced through.

Remove the skillet from the oven and spoon the kimchi mixture over the chicken. Plate and serve immediately.

Skirt Steak Ssam with Kimchi Puree Chimichurri

I wanted to explore a combination of skirt steak marinade with pureed kimchi and Argentine chimichurri sauce. The pungent, garlicky, kimchi puree in the marinade adds layered flavors to the caramelized skirt steak. I've also used flank steak, which is leaner, with great success. You can also use the sauce as the base for *ssamjang* (a sauce for lettuce wraps called *ssam*) mixed with miso paste or *doenjang* (a heartier, fermented Korean soybean paste) to add another dimension to this simple meal. Serve with additional kimchi, rice, and lettuce and you have a complete meal.

› Prep: 20 minutes, plus 24 hours to marinate › Makes 4 to 6 servings

Chimichurri Marinade
3/4 cup any aged napa cabbage kimchi
1/2 cup chopped yellow onion
1/3 cup chopped cilantro
1/2 cup kimchi juice
2 tablespoons minced garlic
3 teaspoons kosher salt

1 (1 1/2-pound) skirt or flank steak
2 teaspoons freshly ground black pepper

Ssamjang
1 tablespoon toasted sesame oil
2 tablespoons yellow mild miso paste or
    Korean doenjang, if available
2 teaspoons Korean chile pepper flakes

2 tablespoons canola oil
Whole pieces of green or red leaf lettuce, leaves
    separated, washed, and dried
Steamed rice, for serving (optional)
2 cups any napa cabbage kimchi, chopped, for
    serving

In a mini food processor fitted with a metal blade, blend together the kimchi, onion, cilantro, kimchi juice, garlic, and 1 teaspoon of the salt. Season the steak on both sides with the remaining salt and the pepper. Pour half of the sauce into a gallon-size resealable bag, place the steak inside, squeeze out the excess air, and seal. Be sure that the marinade is evenly distributed. Marinate in the refrigerator for 24 hours.

In a small bowl, combine the remaining chimichurri sauce with the sesame oil, miso, and chile pepper flakes and refrigerate until ready to serve.

Remove the steak from the refrigerator, discard the marinade, and pat the steak dry to remove as much of the marinade as possible.

Heat the canola oil in a cast-iron skillet over high heat until it shimmers. Add the steak and cook for 4 to 5 minutes per side, depending on how you like your steak. Make sure a nice crust forms.

Let the steak rest for 10 minutes before carving. Slice the meat thinly against the grain. Arrange a few pieces of lettuce on the plate, place the rice on top of the lettuce, then add a few slices of beef, drizzle on the miso sauce, and top with the kimchi.

Braised Short Ribs with Bachelor Radish Kimchi

This recipe calls for searing the meat first rather than following the traditional Korean method of soaking the meat first, boiling off the fat, and then braising. I also wanted to play on the idea of how similar in flavor the Korean bachelor radish is to a turnip, a beloved root vegetable that releases its creamy, delicate, savory liquid while being braised with meat. The slightly tangy broth from the bachelor radish is a contrast to the sweet, caramelized short ribs. The turnips absorb the spicy broth from the bachelor radishes, and the radish tops complement the celery notes. This fusion dish was developed using American-style short ribs as opposed to the traditional Korean cut, but the Korean flavors from the kimchi bring it full circle.

Use well-aged (fermented for more than 4 months in the refrigerator) bachelor radish kimchi to bring out the best flavors in this dish. You may also substitute daikon radish kimchi (page 85) for the Bachelor Radish Kimchi (page 87). Serve with polenta.

› Prep: 3 hours › Makes 4 servings

2 tablespoons neutral cooking oil

3 pounds short ribs on the bone (cut American-style)

1 teaspoon kosher salt

1/4 teaspoon freshly ground black pepper

1 medium onion, diced

2 cloves garlic, sliced

1/2 cup peeled and chopped celery (about 2 stalks)

1 cup chopped carrots (about 2 medium carrots)

1 cup diced turnip (about 1 medium turnip)

6 dried shiitake mushrooms, rehydrated and sliced in half

6 to 8 pieces (with stems) Bachelor Radish Kimchi (page 87)

1/2 cup juice from Bachelor Radish Kimchi (page 87)

1 cup Beef Stock (page 25) or store-bought high-quality low-sodium stock

1/2 cup dry red wine

1 tablespoon yellow mild miso

1/2 Bosc pear, peeled, cored, and pureed

2 tablespoons soy sauce

1 teaspoon sesame oil

Flat-leaf parsley, chopped, for garnish

Position a rack in the middle of the oven and preheat the oven to 350°F.

In a 5-quart Dutch oven set over high heat, heat the cooking oil until it shimmers. Season the ribs with the salt and pepper, add to the pot, and, working in batches if necessary to avoid crowding, brown well on all sides, 12 to 14 minutes. Remove the ribs and set aside.

Reduce the heat to medium-high and add the onion, garlic, celery, carrots, turnip, and mushrooms. Cook, stirring, until the onion is slightly brown, 8 to 10 minutes. Stir in the kimchi and the juice and cook, stirring, until the juice begins to simmer. Add the stock, wine, and miso. Bring to a gentle simmer, then add the ribs. Make sure they are coated

CONTINUED

with the braising liquid but not completely submerged. Continue simmering for 8 to 10 minutes.

In a small bowl, stir together the pear, soy sauce, and sesame oil. Brush the mixture on top of the ribs in the Dutch oven, cover, and place the pot in the oven. Braise for $1^1/_2$ hours, then remove the lid and cook for another 45 minutes, until the meat is tender and falling off the bone.

Transfer the ribs and vegetables to a platter. Bring the braising liquid to a simmer over medium-high heat, skimming off the fat regularly. Reduce the liquid slightly and return the ribs and vegetables to the pot to reheat just until warm. Serve garnished with the parsley.

Kimchi Oven-Baked Baby Back Ribs

Did you know that you can make a barbecue glaze using kimchi juice? The recipe couldn't be simpler. Mike Suppa, the executive chef at Todd English's Plaza Food Hall and a fan of our kimchi, told me about his popular baby back ribs. He collects leftover kimchi juice, marinates the ribs in the juice for two days, and then slow cooks them to perfection. Right before serving, he reduces the juice with sugar for a tangy sweet-and-sour glaze. What you get are delicious, falling-off-the-bone ribs with a hint of delicate kimchi flavor.

› Prep: 4¹/₂ hours, plus 2 days for marinating › Makes 2 main-course servings, 4 appetizer servings

2 pounds baby back ribs
1¹/₂ cups kimchi juice, divided
3 tablespoons sugar
1 teaspoon Korean chile pepper flakes (optional)

Place the ribs in a large resealable bag and add 1¹/₄ cups of the kimchi juice. Squeeze the air out of the bag, seal, and marinate, refrigerated, for 48 hours.

Position a rack in the middle of the oven and preheat the oven to 300°F. Discard the marinade and place the ribs in an ovenproof dish or a roasting pan. Sprinkle the ribs with 1 tablespoon of the sugar. Cover the dish with foil and slow cook the ribs for 3 hours. Check periodically to ensure that the sugar is not burning in the pan. (If you catch the sugar burning, add some water to the pan.) Remove from the oven and transfer the ribs to a plate.

To make the glaze, strain the roasting juices through a fine-mesh strainer into a small pot. Add the remaining kimchi juice, the remaining sugar, and the chile pepper flakes and bring the mixture to a boil. Boil, stirring occasionally, for about 20 minutes, until the juice has thickened and reduced by half. Remove from the heat. Place the ribs back in the baking dish and, using a pastry brush, generously brush the glaze over the ribs. Broil the ribs for 2 minutes, until the glaze is thick and set. Watch the ribs carefully, checking after 1 minute to be sure they aren't charring. Remove from the broiler and allow to rest for 10 minutes. Serve hot or warm.

Kimchi Chigae Stew

This soup is as comforting to me as chicken noodle soup is to so many. In Korea, there is an expression "One eats kimchi to revive one's tired palate." I make *chigae* when I need a little extra comfort in my bowl and it never fails me.

There are many different variations of kimchi *chigae* (simple stew)—the most popular version is made with pork belly. I like to use a simple method of braising the cabbage in olive oil, which allows the combination of olive oil, butter, and the tanginess of kimchi to come to life. Add tofu, rice, and roasted seaweed and you have a nourishing meal. For a truly memorable *chigae*, it's important to use a well-aged (more than 3 months) kimchi so that the developed flavors really shine. Feel free to experiment and add meat—sausage, kielbasa, or even fish. Koreans also commonly add canned mackerel, which is available at Korean markets. Or try it with an oily fresh fish such as canned sardines or whitefish.

▸ Prep: 30 minutes ▸ Makes 4 to 6 servings

1/4 cup extra-virgin olive oil

1/4 cup unsalted butter, divided

2 cups any napa cabbage kimchi, cut into 2-inch pieces

1/2 cup reserved kimchi juice (or water if unavailable)

6 cups water

1 chicken, beef, or vegetarian bouillon cube (the highest quality available), or 3 teaspoons freeze-dried powdered dashi

1 (14-ounce) package medium-firm tofu, cut into 1 1/2-inch cubes

2 green onions, green parts only, cut into 2-inch pieces (optional)

In a 4-quart saucepan over medium-high heat, warm the olive oil and 2 tablespoons of the butter until the mixture shimmers. Add the kimchi and cook for 3 to 4 minutes, until it becomes more translucent.

Add the kimchi juice, decrease the heat to medium, cover, and continue to cook for another 8 to 10 minutes. Open the lid and check on the kimchi to make sure that it is not dry and burning. Keeping the saucepan uncovered, add the water and bring to a boil.

Add the remaining butter and the bouillon cube and stir until well incorporated.

Add the tofu as the stew comes to a boil and continue to cook, uncovered, for 10 minutes, until the tofu is fluffy. Stir in the green onions and cook for 1 minute. Ladle into bowls and serve immediately.

Russian-Inspired Kimchi Schi

The traditions of preserving cabbage as sauerkraut and kimchi come together in this Russian kimchi soup recipe shared by Olga Massov, who helped me write this book. She told me about *schi*, one of the most popular soups in Russia. While there are many versions of *schi*, *kisliye schi* is made with fermented Russian cabbage. Olga took inspiration from her childhood and Russian heritage and reinvented this soup using napa cabbage kimchi in place of fermented Russian "sour" cabbage. Instead of the sour note *kisliye schi* tends to hit, the kimchi adds a layer of spice and heat. The Russian version of Kimchi Chigae Stew (opposite), this soup is brothy, meaty, and flavorful, with a radiant, warming heat that grows with each spoonful—the perfect antidote to cold, snowy winters—and a meal in and of itself. If you prefer, you can make this soup with vegetable stock instead of beef. Of course, no Russian soup is served without sour cream, so a dollop on top of your bowl is just the thing!

› Prep: 2¹/₂ hours › Makes 6 servings

3 tablespoons extra-virgin olive oil

1 pound stew beef, bone-in if possible

2 large cloves garlic, minced

1 small head (1¹/₂ pounds) napa cabbage or ¹/₂ head (1 pound) green cabbage, chopped into 2-inch pieces (about 4 cups)

4 cups Beef Stock (page 25)

4 cups water

3 to 4 cups any cabbage kimchi, cut into ¹/₂-inch pieces

1 (12-ounce) can stewed tomatoes, chopped

2 fresh bay leaves, or 1 dried bay leaf

8 black peppercorns

Kosher salt

Freshly ground black pepper

2 large potatoes (such as Yukon gold), peeled and diced

Sour cream (optional)

In a large stockpot or an 8-quart Dutch oven set over high heat, warm 2 tablespoons of the oil until it shimmers. Add the beef and cook until browned, about 8 minutes. Remove the meat from the pot and set aside.

Reduce the heat to medium and add the garlic to the pot. Cook for 1 minute, then add the cabbage and the remaining 1 tablespoon olive oil. Cook, stirring, until the cabbage has wilted, about 5 minutes.

Add the stock, water, kimchi, browned beef, tomatoes, bay leaves, and peppercorns. Bring to a simmer, cover, reduce the heat to low, and let simmer gently for 1¹/₂ hours. Skim off the floating fat, and season with salt and pepper to taste, taking into account that kimchi contains salt. Add the potatoes and simmer for another 15 to 20 minutes, until the potatoes are fork-tender. Ladle into bowls and top with a dollop of sour cream.

Friulian Bean Soup with Savoy Cabbage Kimchi

When I asked Mindy Fox, an editor at the magazine *La Cucina Italiana*, about an Italian soup that would complement kimchi flavors, she suggested this Friulian soup from Trieste called *jota*, which has been made by farmers for centuries. The soup reflects Trieste's Austrian, Hungarian, and Slovenian culinary influences by marrying together sauerkraut, beans, and pork. I was so happy to discover the wonderful results—it's a rich, hearty soup that's perfect for a winter meal. Its aroma and the combination of earthy beans and kimchi instantly reminded me of miso flavors; this may just be my new favorite Italian soup. Try topping it with fresh baby arugula and Parmigiano-Reggiano just before serving.

› Prep: 2 hours › Makes 6 servings

1¹/₂ pounds bone-in pork chops

1³/₄ cups (about 10 ounces) dried borlotti,
cranberry, or pinto beans, soaked overnight
and drained

2 bay leaves

12 cups cold water

3 tablespoons extra-virgin olive oil

3 ounces pancetta or thick-cut uncured slab
bacon, cut into ¹/₄-inch cubes

1 small yellow onion, coarsely chopped

2 cloves garlic, thinly sliced

2 cups Savoy Cabbage Kimchi with Turnip
(page 80)

3 tablespoons cornmeal

2 teaspoons kosher salt

¹/₂ cup coarsely chopped flat-leaf parsley,
or arugula

Freshly grated Parmigiano-Reggiano (optional)

Remove the bone from the pork chop and cut the pork chop into ¹/₂-inch dice.

In a 5-quart Dutch oven or stockpot over high heat, combine the beans, pork chop bone, pork chop cubes, and bay leaves. Cover with the cold water and bring to a boil. Decrease the heat and let simmer gently, skimming the foam occasionally, until the beans are just tender, about 1 hour. Remove from the heat and discard the bone. Cover the pot to keep warm.

In a large skillet over medium-high heat, warm the oil then cook the pancetta until browned, about 4 minutes. Add the onion and garlic and cook, stirring occasionally, until the onion is softened, about 3 minutes. Add the kimchi and cornmeal and cook, stirring, for 4 minutes more.

Transfer the mixture to the Dutch oven and simmer, covered, stirring occasionally, for about 40 minutes. Add the salt and adjust the seasonings as necessary. Serve hot, garnished with parsley and sprinkled with Parmigiano-Reggiano.

Kimchi Grapefruit Margarita

One of my favorite cocktails is a savory-spicy grapefruit-habanero margarita from Barrio Chino in New York City. The idea of a grapefruit cocktail is simple enough, but using kimchi-infused tequila with a fresh habanero chile makes for a delicious drink. The kimchi notes are brightened by the chile heat and the sweet grapefruit juice; the color reminds me of a Sicilian blood orange. This margarita is perfect for summer barbecues—so you can eat *and* drink your kimchi!

› Prep: 5 minutes, plus 2 hours to infuse   › Makes 4 drinks

1 cup tequila
1/2 fresh habanero pepper
1 cup any napa cabbage kimchi
1 tablespoon kimchi juice
1 1/3 cups fresh pink grapefruit juice
2 slices pink grapefruit, cut in half, for garnish

In a large bowl, combine the tequila, pepper, kimchi, and kimchi juice. Allow the mixture to infuse for at least 2 hours. Strain the tequila into a bowl through a sieve and discard the solids.

Fill 4 glasses with ice cubes. Divide the tequila-grapefruit mixture evenly among the and garnish with grapefruit slices.

Michelada

A refreshing combination of kimchi juice and beer, this take on the classic Michelada is a savory, effervescent drink that tastes like a pickled kimchi kombucha.

Serves 1

1 (12-ounce) lager beer
1/3 cup kimchi juice, strained through a sieve
1/4 teaspoon anchovy sauce
1 teaspoon fresh lime juice

Combine all the ingredients in a chilled 16-ounce beer glass, stir, and enjoy.

Index

Measurement Conversion Charts

Volume

U.S.	Imperial	Metric
1 tablespoon	1/2 fl oz	15 ml
2 tablespoons	1 fl oz	30 ml
1/4 cup	2 fl oz	60 ml
1/3 cup	3 fl oz	90 ml
1/2 cup	4 fl oz	120 ml
2/3 cup	5 fl oz (1/4 pint)	150 ml
3/4 cup	6 fl oz	180 ml
1 cup	8 fl oz (1/3 pint)	240 ml
1 1/4 cups	10 fl oz (1/2 pint)	300 ml
2 cups (1 pint)	16 fl oz (2/3 pint)	480 ml
2 1/2 cups	20 fl oz (1 pint)	600 ml
1 quart	32 fl oz (1 2/3 pint)	1 l

Temperature

Fahrenheit	Celsius/Gas Mark
250°F	120°C/gas mark 1/2
275°F	135°C/gas mark 1
300°F	150°C/gas mark 2
325°F	160°C/gas mark 3
350°F	180 or 175°C/gas mark 4
375°F	190°C/gas mark 5
400°F	200°C/gas mark 6
425°F	220°C/gas mark 7
450°F	230°C/gas mark 8
475°F	245°C/gas mark 9
500°F	260°C

Length

Inch	Metric
1/4 inch	6 mm
1/2 inch	1.25 cm
3/4 inch	2 cm
1 inch	2.5 cm
6 inches (1/2 foot)	15 cm
12 inches (1 foot)	30 cm

Weight

U.S./Imperial	Metric
1/2 oz	15 g
1 oz	30 g
2 oz	60 g
1/4 lb	115 g
1/3 lb	150 g
1/2 lb	225 g
3/4 lb	350 g
1 lb	450 g

Copyright © 2012 by Lauryn Chun
Photographs copyright © 2012 by Sara Remington

Published in the United States by Ten Speed Press, an imprint of the
Crown Publishing Group, a division of Random House, Inc., New York.
www.crownpublishing.com
www.tenspeed.com

Ten Speed Press and the Ten Speed Press colophon are registered trademarks
of Random House, Inc.

Photographs pages 14–15 courtesy Adam Field Pottery

Library of Congress Cataloging-in-Publication Data is on file with the
publisher.

ISBN 978-1-60774-335-4
eISBN 978-1-60774-336-1

Printed in China

Design by Betsy Stromberg
Food styling by Katie Christ
Prop styling by Jaimi Holker

10 9 8 7 6 5 4 3 2 1

First Edition